Bible Secrets Series
Book 2

Angels & Men

HIDDEN MYSTERIES FROM CREATION TO THE TIME OF THE END UNVEILED

M.M. TAUSON
Author of: *THE DEEP THINGS OF GOD*
A Primer on the Secrets of Heaven and Earth

ANGELS & MEN
**Hidden Mysteries from Creation
to the Time of the End Unveiled**

Copyright © 2014 by Maximiano Maximo Tuason, Jr.

All rights reserved. Use of the literature contained herein is encouraged. However, to protect the integrity of its contents, this book, whether as a whole or in part, except for brief excerpts in reviews, may not be reproduced in any form without the written permission of the publisher.

First printing: July 2014

ISBN 978-971-95293-1-6

Unless otherwise specified, Scripture quotations are from the Authorized King James Version (KJV) of the Bible.

Published by:
BAYITH HA-SHEM PUBLICATIONS
P.O. Box 3272, Makati City, 1200 Philippines
email: bayithashem@yahoo.com

Contents

Preface

1. Angels Up Close and Personal   1

2. The Roles Angels Play   17

3. Rebels and Renegades   31

4. Battleground Earth!   49

5. The Heirs of Heaven   71

6. Man's Manual for Survival   99

7. Secrets of the Soul and Spirit   131

8. The Light of Eternal Life   153

Appendix   165

Endnotes   166

To the Father,

For my Brethren

Preface

When I wrote Volume I of this Bible Secrets Series (*The Deep Things of God: A Primer on the Secrets of Heaven and Earth*), I thought to myself that, if it could help enlighten even just one soul, I would be fulfilled. From the reactions to and comments about that first book that have reached me, it looks like I have surpassed my goal a few times over. And, so, as originally planned, this Book 2.

Some people are incredulous that secrets can still be discovered in the Scriptures. They say, "Have not all their contents been studied, analyzed, and interpreted countless times for nearly 2,000 years since apostolic times?" (Actually, over 4,000 years -- since about 2100 BC, some 250 years after Noah's Flood, when the oldest book of the Bible – that of Job – was written.)

But Biblical revelation is apparently a continuing process for the perfection of the faithful. Moses tells us, *"The secret things belong unto the LORD our God: but those things which are revealed belong unto us and to our children for ever, that we may do all the words of this law"* (Deut 29:29).

The late prophecy watchman-publisher J.R. Church wrote in an article entitled "Home of the Soul" in *Prophecy in the News* (March 1999, p. 10): "The many discoveries that have been made in the Scriptures over the past century can only be described as a type of reverse engineering. Theologians are actually 'reverse-engineering' a Divine document, written over a period of 1,500 years, the last of which was written 2,000 years ago, and are finding incredible designs that could not have been produced by mere humans."

Divine revelation, prophecy says, will continue until the very time of the end. *"But in the days of the voice of the seventh angel, when he shall begin to sound, the mystery of God should be finished, as he hath declared to his servants the prophets"* (Revelation 10:7).

The conclusions presented in this book have been arrived at through simple deductive logic – from bits and pieces of

Scripture that, when placed together, bring to light a big picture and erstwhile hidden Biblical truths.

The premises are based solely on Scriptures – that is, Sola Scriptura, or only the Bible – and both the Old and New Testaments. We need both. We cannot get the whole picture without one or the other. As the prophet Isaiah said, *"To the law* (Old Testament) *and to the testimony* (New Testament)*: if they speak not according to this word, it is because there is no light* (truth) *in them"* (Isa 8:20).

The text is occasionally complemented with information from science, history, and current events, as well as brief excerpts from extra-Biblical references, such as Josephus, Jewish commentaries, the Book of Enoch – but only when these do not contradict Scriptural tenets, but rather supply additional details for the reader's clearer understanding.

Some readers wonder why I frequently refer to Jewish writings and traditions. Let us allow the apostle Peter to explain. *"What advantage, then, is there in being a Jew, or what value is there in circumcision? Much in every way! First of all, they have been entrusted with the very words of God"* (Romans 3:1-2, NIV). Christ Himself sums it up neatly. *"You Samaritans worship what you do not know; we worship what we do know, for salvation is from the Jews"* (John 4:22, NIV).

When I was taking up Homiletics in Bible school, our teacher used to advise us to avoid, among the common forms of sermon, the topical type, it being the most difficult and least focused. This series, though, as demanded by its nature, has to be presented as a compendium of topical Bible studies strung together in printed format.

May this book serve as a roadmap for you on your journey to the kingdom of heaven. Godspeed!

M.M. TAUSON

1

Angels Up Close and Personal

Whereas angels, which are greater in power and might...

-- 2 Peter 2:11a

What are angels? Where did they come from? When did they come into existence? Our primary source of information about them is the Judeo-Christian Scriptures, the Bible.

The word "angel" is the English transliteration of the Greek term *aggelos* (pronounced "angelos"), which is a translation of the Hebrew word *malakh* meaning "messenger."

Origin and nature of angels

The Bible has it on record that God simply spoke to create the angels: *"By the word of the LORD were the heavens made, their starry host by the breath of his mouth"* (Ps 33:6, NIV).

The composer of Psalm 148:1-5 confirms that the host (army) of angels has been created by divine command. *"Praise ye the LORD. Praise ye the LORD from the heavens: praise him in the heights. Praise ye him, all his angels: praise ye him, all his hosts. Praise ye him, sun and moon: praise him, all ye stars of light. Praise him, ye heavens of heavens, and ye waters that be above the heavens. Let them praise the name of the LORD: for he commanded, and they were created."*

We learn from the oldest book of the Bible, Job (38:4, 7), that the angels were created before God formed the earth. *"Where wast thou when I laid the foundations of the earth? declare, if thou hast understanding... When the morning stars sang together, and all the sons of God shouted for joy?"*

(Take note that there were more than one "morning star." Moreover, the phrase "sons of God" refers to and is widely understood to mean the angels, not human beings.)

The angels have been created superior to men, who were formed much, much later. We read in 2 Peter 2:11a, *"Whereas angels, which are greater in power and might..."* Greater than who? Apparently, men – as a psalmist sang hundreds of years before Peter – *"What is man, that thou art mindful of him? and the son of man, that thou visitest him? For thou hast made him a little lower than the angels...:"* (Ps 8:4-5a).

Even Christ, in His incarnation as a mortal man, was in the flesh physically inferior to angels. *"But we see Jesus, who was made a little lower than the angels for the suffering of death, crowned with glory and honour; that he by the grace of God should taste death for every man"* (Heb 2:9).

Angels are spirits

The book of Hebrews says the angels are spirits by nature. The Spirit of God, however, manifested first in the newly created universe. *"In the beginning God created the heaven and the earth. And the earth was without form, and void; and darkness was upon the face of the deep. And the Spirit of God moved upon the face of the waters"* (Gen 1:1-2).

The angels were created subsequently as spirits just like God's Spirit. *"And of the angels he saith, Who maketh his angels spirits, and his ministers a flame of fire"* (Heb 1:7).

What is spirit? Eliphaz the Temanite, a friend of Job, described his encounter with a spirit: *"Then a spirit passed before my face; the hair of my flesh stood up"* (Job 4:15).

The man had goose pimples – something we experience in the presence of static electricity. Thus, a spirit seems to be a form of electricity or electromagnetic energy. In that connection, what is energy? Scientists and industrialists are able to measure, manage, and put energy to use for the benefit of mankind, but nobody seems to know what it really is.

Angels are light

The author of the book of James, probably the Messiah's half-brother, says in an indirect manner that the angels are light. *"Every good gift and every perfect gift is from above, and cometh down from the Father of lights, with whom is no variableness, neither shadow of turning"* (James 1:17).

The angels likely became beings of light after God brought light into existence in the universe. As Moses, the writer of the first five books of the Bible, relates, *"And God said, Let there be light: and there was light"* (Gen 1:3).

Speed of light. Light, modern science teaches, has a velocity of some 186,000 miles (300,000 km.) per second, the fastest in the universe. Scientists say the speed of light is the cosmic speed limit -- nothing can travel faster than light. According to the theories of relativity advanced by Albert Einstein, time stops at the speed of light.

This explains an enigmatic passage in the book of Judges: *"They fought from heaven; the stars in their courses fought against Sisera"* (Judg 5:20). Moving at the speed of light, angels in the stars helped the Israelites win their battle against the Canaanites. Each of their movements forward to earth, then back again to the stars, presumably took just one second or less!

The angels can also communicate from heaven with men on earth in no time at all. *"And the angel of the LORD called unto him out of heaven, and said, Abraham, Abraham: and he said, Here am I.* (Gen 22:11).

The devil, too? Satan, a.k.a. Lucifer, was a special angel of God before ambition brought about his fall. He still possesses some angelic abilities. *"And no marvel; for Satan himself is transformed into an angel of light"* (2 Cor 11:14).

Tempting Christ, who had just fasted forty days and nights in the wilderness, Satan moved at the speed of light. *"And the devil, taking him up into an high mountain, shewed unto him all the kingdoms of the world in a moment of time"* (Luke 4:5). It took Satan just one second to show Christ all those great cities!

Angels are the stars

The angels are often called "stars." *"The seven stars are the angels of the seven churches"* (Rev 1:20b). Hence, we can see angels everyday. All we have to do is look up to the sky at night.

The psalmist exhorts angels to pay homage to God. *"Praise ye him, sun and moon: praise him, all ye stars of light"* (Ps 148:3). If they are merely inanimate heavenly bodies and not intelligent beings, how can the stars praise God?

We also read in Isaiah 14:13 -- *"For thou hast said in thine heart, I will ascend into heaven, I will exalt my throne above the stars of God."* By "stars" are meant the angels; Lucifer wanted to be higher in stature than all the other angels in heaven. .

Moreover, in Revelation 12:4a -- *"And his tail drew the third part of the stars of heaven, and did cast them to the earth..."* Bible teachers generally say that the verse means Satan seduced one-third of the angels, the stars of heaven, into following him.

Angelic names.

God gave every angel and star their own names. *"He telleth the number of the stars; he calleth them all by their names"* (Ps 147:4). The pseudepigraphal Book of Enoch has something similar to say "I beheld another splendour, and the stars of heaven. I observed that he called them all by their respective names, and that they heard. In a righteous balance I saw that he weighed out with their light the amplitude of their places, and the day of their appearance, and their conversion. Splendour produced splendour; and their conversion was into the number of the angels, and of the faithful."[1]

The writer gives us the additional information that God can tell by their radiance the sizes ("amplitude") of the stars, as well as the time of their creation and transformation into light. And their number is the same as the number of the angels and of the faithful believers on earth!

Only three angels are named in the King James Version (KJV): the archangel Michael (Jude 9, etc.), whose name means "who is like God?" in Hebrew; the angel Gabriel (Luke 1:19, etc.), with a name signifying "God's hero"; and the fallen angel Lucifer (Isa 14:12), whose name, though, is not really a name, but a coined Latin epithet meaning "light-bearer."

Do all angels have wings?

In religious paintings and church frescoes, angels are often depicted as either children or adult human beings with wings. This seems to be the result of the description in Scriptures of angels being able to fly. *"...while I was still in prayer, Gabriel, the man I had seen in the earlier vision, came to me in swift flight about the time of the evening sacrifice"* (Dan 9:21-22, NIV). This is seen in both the Old and New Testaments – *"And I saw another angel fly in the midst of heaven, having the everlasting gospel to preach unto them that dwell on the earth, and to every nation, and kindred, and tongue, and people"* (Rev 14:6) So, do all angels have wings?

Men without wings. Angels also manifest to people as men without wings. They visited Abraham in human form. *"And he lift up his eyes and looked, and, lo, three men stood by him: and when he saw them, he ran to meet them from the tent door, and bowed himself toward the ground"* (Gen 18:2).

Much later, Abraham's grandson Jacob would wrestle with an angel who appeared as a man. *"And Jacob was left alone; and there wrestled a man with him until the breaking of the day"* (Gen 32:24).

A man came to announce Samson's birth to his childless parents. *"Then the woman came and told her husband, saying, A man of God came unto me, and his countenance was like the countenance of an angel of God, very terrible"* (Judg 13:6a).

The angel Gabriel appeared as a man to explain Daniel's prophetic visions: *"And it came to pass, when I, even I Daniel, had seen the vision, and sought for the meaning, then, behold, there stood before me as the appearance of a man. And I heard a man's voice between the banks of Ulai, which called, and said, Gabriel, make this man to understand the vision"* (Dan 8:15-16).

Two men, obviously angels, appeared to the disciples as Christ ascended to heaven. *"And while they looked stedfastly toward heaven as he went up, behold, two men stood by them in white apparel"* (Acts 1:10-ff.).

In Hebrews, Paul advises us to be hospitable even to people we do not know, they could be angels! *"Be not forgetful to entertain strangers: for thereby some have entertained angels unawares"* (Heb 13:2). Not all angels have wings.

Angels are immortal

Angels possess eternal life. Christ implied this much when referring to the people who will gain entry into the kingdom of heaven, *"Neither can they die any more: for they are equal unto the angels; and are the children of God, being the children of the resurrection."* (Luke 20:36). Angels do not die.

As beings of light, angels are made up of photons, which quantum physicists say can travel to and fro, and all around the universe indefinitely. Photons, just like all particles with no mass, are able to negotiate vast distances without any loss of energy. They thus endure infinitely in time and space. So, too, angels.

Are angels male and female?

Most religious portrayals of angels by artists, specially in Medieval and Renaissance times, present them as youths with fine features, almost feminine in appearance. Yet, the texts about angels in the Bible, including their names, are masculine.

Some cite the following passage in Zechariah as proof that there are female angels. *"Then lifted I up mine eyes, and looked, and, behold, there came out two women, and the wind was in their wings; for they had wings like the wings of a stork: and they lifted up the ephah between the earth and the heaven..."*

But the stork is an "unclean" bird (Lev 11:13,19; Deut 14:18). Would God have given any angel such wings? The issue is clarified in two earlier lines: *"...and this is a woman that sitteth in the midst of the ephah. And he said, This is wickedness"* (Zech 5:9,7b-8a). The *ephah* (a large container for measuring grain) had a wicked woman in it (prophetic symbol of a sinful religion). So, the two women with stork-like wings were not actually angels, but representations of pagan churches and their worshippers.

Angels do not multiply. The angels seem to have just one gender. *"For in the resurrection they neither marry, nor are given in marriage, but are as the angels of God in heaven"* (Matt 22:30). They do not marry to reproduce, so it looks like angels have only one sex. Besides, they are called "sons of God" (Job 38:7, etc.), so they must all be male. The disobedient angels who came down to earth to have sexual relations with the daughters of men were "sons of God" (Gen 6:2). (More on this later.)

Original gender. Hebrew, the original language God and Adam used to speak with each other, proves that the male was the first and original gender. We first see the word "female" in Genesis 1:27 when God created man – *"male and female created he them."* The Hebrew word for "female" is *neqebah*, from the root-word *naqab*, which means "to puncture, perforate,"[2] that is, to put a hole in, obviously for child-bearing in females. So, from the definition, it looks like the female was merely a modification of the male of the species, and the angels, who were God's first created living beings, are all male.

Bearded men? When angels manifested as men, were they seen as bearded male grownups? Christ said the saved will be "as the angels" in heaven. Since God forbids male Israelites (His chosen people) to shave their side-whiskers or even trim their beards (Lev 19:27; 21:5), the angels are probably bearded, too! How can the saved be like the angels in heaven if they have beards, while the angels have bare faces?

Are angels all-knowing?

Many people regard angels as just a cut below God, who is omniscient, and so think that they must be all-knowing, too. But the Scriptures belie this. We read in Matthew 24:36: *"But of that day and hour knoweth no man, no, not the angels of heaven, but my Father only."* The angels do not know when Christ will return. They are not privy to the thoughts of the Father.

And in 1 Peter 1:12 (NKJV), *"To them it was revealed that, not to themselves, but to us they were ministering the things which now have been reported to you through those who have preached the gospel to you by the Holy Spirit sent from heaven -- things which angels desire to look into."* The angels, who had been bypassed by the Holy Spirit, wanted to know the things revealed to the disciples!

In fact, according to Ephesians 3:10 (NIV), God's plans were communicated to angelic leaders only through the assembly of believers. *"His intent was that now, through the church, the manifold wisdom of God should be made known to the rulers and authorities in the heavenly realms."*

The verses show that neither angels nor demons can read our minds. Yet, that should not make us complacent. They probably know how to interpret our thoughts and intentions from our body language and other physical signs, such as eye movement, heartbeat, body temperature, perspiration, etc. After all, they have had thousands of years to master these skills.

Angels not worshipped

Apostate Israelites worshipped the stars (2 Kings 21:1-3; Zeph 1:4-5), which we have seen are the angels themselves. But Paul warns us: *"Let no man beguile you of your reward in a voluntary humility and worshipping of angels, intruding into those things which he hath not seen, vainly puffed up by his fleshly mind"* (Col 2:18).

Despite this, John attempted to worship the angel who spoke to him. *"Then the angel said to me, 'Write:' At this I fell at his feet to worship him. But he said to me, 'Do not do it! I am a fellow servant with you and with your brothers who hold to the testimony of Jesus. Worship God!'"* (Rev 19:10a).

A bit later, he tried to do it again. *"And I John saw these things, and heard them. And when I had heard and seen, I fell down to worship before the feet of the angel which shewed me these things. Then saith he unto me, See thou do it not: for I am thy fellowservant, and of thy brethren the prophets, and of them which keep the sayings of this book: worship God"* (Rev 22:8-9).

Kinds of angels

It may surprise some people to know that angels come in different kinds and forms. Let us focus on each kind.

Cherubim.

When we see or hear the word "cherubim" or "cherubs," what images immediately come to our minds? Yes, little winged children – although in Hebrew, the origin of the word is unknown. In Arabic, a sister-tongue of Hebrew, *ker rubh* means "like a youth." This probably contributed to the depiction of cherubim as little children with wings.

There is, however, no such description of cherubs in the Bible. That picture is a far cry from the image we get when cherubim were first mentioned in the Scriptures. *"So he drove out the man; and he placed at the east of the garden of Eden*

Cherubims, and a flaming sword which turned every way, to keep the way of the tree of life" (Gen 3:24). Cherubs are shown here as guards with a flaming sword, prepared to prevent trespassers, obviously by force if necessary, from entering the Garden of Eden.

Four faces and wings. Ezekiel saw a strangely different vision of cherubs: *"And every one had four faces, and every one had four wings... Thus were their faces: and their wings were stretched upward; two wings of every one were joined one to another, and two covered their bodies"* (Ezek 1:6,11). Here, we discover that the cherubs have four faces and four wings!

Covered with eyes. What is more... *"And their whole body, and their backs, and their hands, and their wings, and the wheels, were full of eyes round about, even the wheels that they four had"* (Ezek 10:12-14). The cherubs were covered all over with eyes! What could be the reason for that?

Seraphim.

Another class of angels is made up of what are known as "seraphs" or "seraphim." In Hebrew, *seraphim* means "fiery, burning ones," from the root-word *seraph*, signifying "to burn, be on fire." However, the German Biblical critic Wilhelm Gesenius connects it with the Arab. term *shrafa* meaning "high" or "exalted."[3]

Six wings. In the book of Isaiah, we read that seraphs have six wings. *"In the year that king Uzziah died I saw also the Lord sitting upon a throne, high and lifted up, and his train filled the temple. Above it stood the seraphims: each one had six wings; with twain he covered his face, and with twain he covered his feet, and with twain he did fly. And one cried unto another, and said, Holy, holy, holy, is the LORD of hosts: the whole earth is full of his glory."* (Isa 6:1-3).

The four creatures around the throne of God in heaven look like they are seraphs. *"And before the throne there was a sea of glass like unto crystal: and in the midst of the throne, and round about the throne, were four beasts full of eyes before and behind. And the first beast was like a lion, and the second beast like a calf, and the third beast had a face as a man, and the fourth beast was like a flying eagle. And the four beasts had each* of them six wings about him; and they were full of eyes within: and they rest not day and night, saying, Holy, holy, holy, Lord God Almighty, which was, and is, and is to come"* (Rev 4:6-8).

The four also have six wings and likewise tirelessly chant "Holy, holy, holy." Both cherubs and seraphs are said to be "full of eyes." They closely resemble the next class of angels.

Watchers.

We first see "watchers" in the OT book of Daniel. *"I saw in the visions of my head upon my bed, and, behold, a watcher and an holy one came down from heaven... This matter is by the decree of the watchers, and the demand by the word of the holy ones: to the intent that the living may know that the most High ruleth in the kingdom of men, and giveth it to whomsoever he will, and setteth up over it the basest of men... And whereas the king saw a watcher and an holy one coming down from heaven"* (Dan 4:13,17,23).

Of course, the question that immediately comes to mind is, why are they called "watchers"? Is it because they are "full of eyes" all over their persons?

Watchers seem to form a highly privileged class of angels. They are almost always in the presence of God. In Revelation 4:6 in the preceding page: *"And before the throne there was a sea of glass like unto crystal: and in the midst of the throne, and round about the throne, were four beasts full of eyes before and behind."* Who do they watch with their numerous eyes? The clue probably lies in the appearance of their faces.

Four faces. Four angels were also with God in a vision the prophet Ezekiel saw. *"Also out of the midst thereof came the likeness of four living creatures. And this was their appearance; they had the likeness of a man. And every one had four faces, and every one had four wings... As for the likeness of their faces, they four had the face of a man, and the face of a lion, on the right side: and they four had the face of an ox on the left side; they four also had the face of an eagle"* (Ezek 1:5-6,10)

They are very similar the four seraphim around the throne of God. *"And the first beast was like a lion, and the second beast like a calf, and the third beast had a face as a man, and the fourth beast was like a flying eagle"* (Rev 4:7).

Four kinds of creature. Curiously, their four faces are the likenesses of four of the six kinds of creature that God created on the fifth and sixth days of creation: "fowl" or flying animals (eagle), "beasts of the earth" or wild animals (lion), "cattle" or domesticated animals (calf or ox), and man (Gen 1:21-26). The obvious implication? The watchers must be the overseers or caretakers of the creatures on earth that they resemble!

Only two kinds of creature -- water animals and creeping things -- have no look-alike watchers over them. The Scriptures assert this: *"And makest men as the fishes of the sea, as the creeping things, that have no ruler over them?"* (Hab 1:14).

Holy ones.

In the prophetic dream of King Nebuchadnezzar of Babylon: *"I saw in the visions of my head upon my bed, and, behold, a watcher and an holy one came down from heaven"* (Dan 4:13). The identity of the "holy one" is a deep mystery.

Twenty-four elders? Some Bible commentators say the "holy one" is one of the twenty-four elders around the throne of God that we read about in Revelation 4:4,10-11 -- *"And round about the throne were four and twenty seats: and upon the seats I saw four and twenty elders sitting, clothed in white raiment; and they had on their heads crowns of gold... The four and twenty elders fall down before him that sat on the throne, and worship him that liveth for ever and ever, and cast their crowns before the throne, saying, Thou art worthy, O Lord, to receive glory and honour and power: for thou hast created all things, and for thy pleasure they are and were created."*

According to *Fausset's Bible Dictionary:* "The four and twenty elders (Rev 4) represent the combined heads of the Old and New Testament congregations, the twelve patriarchs and twelve apostles; answering to the typical 24 courses of priests, 'governors of the sanctuary and governors of God' (1 Chron 24:5; 25:31)."[4]

However, the lineup of the patriarchs -- the twelve sons of Jacob who became the founders of the twelve tribes of Israel – is uncertain, because in Revelation 7:5-8 the tribe of Dan is replaced by the half-tribe of Manasseh. The same is true for the twelve apostles, inasmuch as in Acts 1:15-26 the traitor Judas was replaced with Matthias and, later, Christ called Paul to be an apostle as well (Acts 9:1-31).

One and the same? Other Bible scholars have different ideas. We read in *Barnes' Notes*: "[And, behold, a watcher and an holy one] Or rather, perhaps, 'even a holy one;' or, 'who was a holy one.' He evidently does not intend to refer to two beings, a 'watcher,' and 'one who was holy;' but he means to designate the character of the watcher, that he was holy, or that he was one of the class of 'watchers' who were ranked as holy... So Bertholdt, 'not two, but only one, who was both a watcher, and was holy; one of those known as watchers and as holy ones'."[5]

We learn further that "and," translated from the Hebrew *waw* [w-], may be used "to denote not an additional one or thing, but to specify something in addition to, or in explanation of" a preceding noun. Thus, in 1 Sam 28:3: "In Ramah, EVEN [w¦- in his own city." 1 Sam 17:40: "And put them in a shepherd's bag which he had, EVEN [w¦-] in a scrip.[6] In short, the "watcher" and the "holy one" are one and the same person.

Archangel.

In the entire KJV, only one angel is identified as an archangel. *"Yet Michael the archangel, when contending with the devil he disputed about the body of Moses, durst not bring against him a railing accusation, but said, The Lord rebuke thee"* (Jude 9). As we already know, "angel" means messenger. The prefix "arch-" comes from the Greek *archein* or *arche*, which signifies "first," "chief," or "principal" – hence, first in order, rank, or power.

Prince or ruler. In a prophecy in Daniel 12:1a -- Gabriel said that the archangel Michael is the head or ruler of the Jews. *"And at that time shall Michael stand up, the great prince which standeth for the children of thy people..."* The Hebrew word translated "prince" is *sar*, which means "head person." Gabriel repeated it a few verses later: *"But I will shew thee that which is noted in the scripture of truth: and there is none that holdeth with me in these things, but Michael your prince"* (Dan 10:21).

It appears that the archangel Michael will be with Christ at the first resurrection or "Rapture" at Christ's Second Coming: *"For the Lord himself shall descend from heaven with a shout, with the voice of the archangel, and with the trump of God: and the dead in Christ shall rise first"* (1 Thess 4:16).

Angel of the LORD.
We all know that Adam and Eve talked with God in the Garden of Eden (Genesis 2-3). Before the Flood, God spoke to Noah about the coming deluge that would destroy the earth and instructed him on how to save himself and his family (Gen ch. 6-7). In Canaan, *"the LORD made a covenant with Abram, saying, Unto thy seed have I given this land, from the river of Egypt unto the great river, the river Euphrates"* (Gen 15:18). Several years later, God tested Abraham when He asked him to sacrifice his son Isaac to Him.

In Exodus, the LORD spoke many times to Moses: -- from the burning bush in the desert of Horeb, telling him to lead the Israelites out of Egypt; through his subsequent dealings with the obstinate Pharaoh and the ten plagues inflicted upon the Egyptians, through Israel's final departure from Egypt, through the giving of the two tablets of law on Mount Sinai, where the people heard the thunderous voice of the LORD, through the forty-year wandering of the Israelites in the wilderness.

We even read in Exodus 33:11 -- *"And the LORD spake unto Moses face to face, as a man speaketh unto his friend."*

Unseen and unheard? It certainly comes as a big surprise, therefore, when the apostle tells us in John 1:18 -- *"No man hath seen God at any time; the only begotten Son, which is in the bosom of the Father, he hath declared him."* Christ reiterates this in John 5:37 -- *"And the Father himself, which hath sent me, hath borne witness of me. Ye have neither heard his voice at any time, nor seen his shape."* If we are to believe John, and we do, then who did Adam and Eve, Noah, Abraham, and Moses talk with?

The incident wherein Jacob wrestled with an angel gives us an idea. *"So Jacob was left alone, and a man wrestled with him till daybreak... Then the man said, 'Your name will no longer be Jacob, but Israel, because you have struggled with God and with men and have overcome.'... So Jacob called the place Peniel, saying, 'It is because I saw God face to face, and yet my life was spared.'"* (Gen 32:24,28,30, NIV).

The *International Standard Bible Encyclopaedia* explains: "Jacob wrestles with the angel and says, 'I have seen God face to face'....Jacob speaks of God and the angel as identical."[7] The angel was the representative of God in physical form.

Divine proxy. In other passages, this divine proxy is called the "angel of the LORD." He appeared to Hagar: *"The angel of the LORD also said to her: 'You are now with child and you will have a son. You shall name him Ishmael, for the LORD has heard of your misery... She gave this name to the LORD who spoke to her: "You are the God who sees me," for she said, "I have now seen the One who sees me"* (Gen 16:11,13, NIV). Notice that Hagar called the angel "God."

To Gideon, *"the angel of the LORD appeared unto him, and said unto him, The LORD is with thee, thou mighty man of valour... And the LORD looked upon him, and said, Go in this thy might, and thou shalt save Israel from the hand of the Midianites: have not I sent thee?"* (Judg 6:12,14). The angel refers to himself as "the LORD" or God Himself!

As we saw earlier, God's angel announced the forthcoming birth of Samson to his barren parents. *"But the angel of the LORD did no more appear to Manoah and to his wife. Then Manoah knew that he was an angel of the LORD. And Manoah said unto his wife, We shall surely die, because we have seen God"* (Judg 13:21-22). The parents-to-be knew he was an angel, and yet they called him God!

When God destroyed Sodom and Gomorrah, there were two "LORDs" – one in mid-air and the other in heaven above. *"Then the LORD rained upon Sodom and upon Gomorrah brimstone and fire from the LORD out of heaven"* (Gen 19:24). The LORD below was the angel of the higher LORD in heaven.

The Son of God? Many commentators speculate that, in some appearances, the "angel of the LORD" is Christ Himself, the Son of God. According to *Nelson's Illustrated Bible Dictionary*, "His similarities to Jesus lead most scholars to conclude that He is the pre-incarnate Word present with God at the creation of the world (John 1:1,14)."[8]

In one instance, Nebuchadnezzar had the Jewish captives Shadrach, Meshach, and Abednego thrown into a furnace for refusing to worship the golden image he had set up. But when he looked, *"Lo, I see four men loose, walking in the midst of the fire, and they have no hurt; and the form of the fourth is like the Son of God"* (Dan 3:25b). The three faithful Jews were saved by an angel who looked like the Son of God!

Joshua, Moses's assistant and successor, met the angel of the LORD. *"And it came to pass, when Joshua was by Jericho, that he lifted his eyes and looked, and behold, a Man stood opposite him with His sword drawn in His hand. And Joshua went to Him and said to Him, 'Are You for us or for our adversaries?' So He said, 'No, but as Commander of the army of the LORD I have now come.' And Joshua fell on his face to the earth and worshiped, and said to Him, 'What does my Lord say to His servant?' Then the Commander of the LORD's army said to Joshua, 'Take your sandal off your foot, for the place where you stand is holy.' And Joshua did so"* (Josh 5:13-15, NKJV).

Only God is worshipped, not angels. Yet, the Angel did not restrain Joshua from worshipping Him. Since the Commander of the LORD's army is not God Himself, he must have been the Son of God!

Power to pardon sin. God told Moses in the wilderness, *"Behold, I send an Angel before thee, to keep thee in the way, and to bring thee into the place which I have prepared. Beware of him, and obey his voice, provoke him not; for he will not pardon your transgressions: for my name is in him"* (Ex 23:20-21). From this passage, we gather that the Angel has the power to pardon sins. According to the *International Standard Bible Encyclopaedia*, "the angel can forgive sin, which only God can do, because God's name, i.e. His character and thus His authority, are in the angel."[9]

The Angel has the name of the LORD in him. It sounds like Christ's own declaration in John 5:43a -- *"I am come in my Father's name…"*

Angelic hierarchy

Angels belong to a well-ordered organization with different ranks and levels. This much we gather from the epistles of the apostles. *"For I am persuaded, that neither death, nor life, nor angels, nor principalities, nor powers, nor things present, nor things to come…"* (Rom 8:38). *"Who is gone into heaven, and is on the right hand of God; angels and authorities and powers being made subject unto him"* (1 Peter 3:22; cf. Eph 3:10, 6:12; Col 2:15; Titus 3:1).

It appears that the angels have been ordained into their respective ranks and positions from creation. *"For by him were all things created, that are in heaven, and that are in earth, visible and invisible, whether they be thrones, or dominions, or principalities, or powers: all things were created by him, and for him"* (Col 1:16). As inferred from their rankings, angels possess different levels of power. What could their respective roles be?

Choirs of angels? There is an esoteric teaching that there are "nine choirs of angels. Arranged according to their importance, in descending order these choirs are the seraphim, cherubim, thrones, dominions, virtues, powers, principalities, archangels, and angels."[10] This concept, however, has no Biblical basis.

Positions and powers? In the book *Angels: From Genesis to Revelation*, we are told that "Louis Sperry Chafer, a noted theologian, gives several good definitions: 'Thrones' refer to 'those who sat upon them.' 'Dominions' refer to 'those who rule.' 'Principalities' refer to 'those who govern.' 'Powers' refer to 'those who exercise supremacy,' and 'authorities' refer to 'those invested with imperial responsibility.'"[11] These definitions, though, like the "nine choirs of angels," are similarly mere products of speculation, with no scriptural support.

2

The Roles Angels Play

Praise the LORD, all his heavenly hosts, you his servants who do his will.

-- Psalm 103:21, NIV.

Why did God create angels? What is the purpose of their existence? What do they do? And, since men have been created like them, what is the relationship between them?

Servants of the Creator

Angels, together with all other things in the universe, have been brought into existence for the Creator's gratification. *"Thou art worthy, O Lord, to receive glory and honour and power: for thou hast created all things, and for thy pleasure they are and were created"* (Rev 4:11).

As the creation of God, the angels must first and foremost worship and praise God. *"Praise ye the LORD. Praise ye the LORD from the heavens: praise him in the heights. Praise ye him, all his angels: praise ye him, all his hosts"* (Ps 148:1-2).

They are servants of God who obey and serve Him at all times. *"Praise the LORD, all his heavenly hosts, you his servants who do his will"* (Ps 103:21, NIV). Christ alluded to this in the model prayer He taught the disciples. *"Thy kingdom come. Thy will be done in earth, as it is in heaven"* (Matt 6:10).

Some angels volunteer unusual services to God. The prophet Michaiah recounted his vision to Ahab, king of Israel. *"I saw the LORD sitting on his throne, and all the host of heaven standing by him on his right hand and on his left. And the LORD said, Who shall persuade Ahab, that he may go up and fall at Ramoth-gilead? And one said on this manner, and another said on that manner. And there came forth a spirit, and stood before the LORD, and said, I will persuade him"* (1 Kings 22:19-21).

Heralds of good news

Some of the most welcome appearances of angels are as messengers of good tidings – many times the birth of personages who helped shape the destiny of the Hebrew nation.

Birth of Isaac.

God, represented by an angel, promised Abraham the birth of a son by his wife Sarah in their old age. *"And God said, Sarah thy wife shall bear thee a son indeed; and thou shalt call his name Isaac: and I will establish my covenant with him for an everlasting covenant, and with his seed after him"* (Gen 17:19).

Birth of Samson.

The angel of the LORD visited the barren wife of Manoah, the father-to-be of Samson, to announce a soon-coming son. *"And the angel of the LORD appeared unto the woman, and said unto her, Behold now, thou art barren, and bearest not: but thou shalt conceive, and bear a son"* (Judg 13:3).

Birth of John.

In the case of John the Baptist, it was the angel Gabriel who told his father, the priest Zacarias, the answer to his prayers. *"And there appeared unto him an angel of the Lord standing on the right side of the altar of incense. And when Zacharias saw him, he was troubled, and fear fell upon him. But the angel said unto him, Fear not, Zacharias: for thy prayer is heard; and thy wife Elisabeth shall bear thee a son, and thou shalt call his name John"* (Luke 1:11-13).

Birth of Christ.

Gabriel was the same angel who announced to the virgin Mary her having been chosen as the future mother of the Messiah. *"And in the sixth month the angel Gabriel was sent from God unto a city of Galilee, named Nazareth, To a virgin espoused to a man whose name was Joseph, of the house of David; and the virgin's name was Mary... And the angel said unto her, Fear not, Mary: for thou hast found favour with God. And, behold, thou shalt conceive in thy womb, and bring forth a son, and shalt call his name JESUS.' He shall be great, and shall be called the Son of the Highest: and the Lord God shall give unto him the throne of his father David"* (Luke 1:26-27,31-32).

It was the angel of the LORD, though, who broke the good news to the shepherds. *"And there were in the same country shepherds abiding in the field, keeping watch over their flock by night... And the angel said unto them, Fear not: for, behold, I bring you good tidings of great joy, which shall be to all people. For unto you is born this day in the city of David a Saviour, which is Christ the Lord. And this shall be a sign unto you; Ye shall find the babe wrapped in swaddling clothes, lying in a manger. And suddenly there was with the angel a multitude of the heavenly host praising God, and saying, Glory to God in the highest, and on earth peace, good will toward men"* (Luke 2:8,10-14).

Defenders of Israel

For the survival of God's holy nation, the angels fought against the enemies of Israel. Let us look at several instances.

Against Canaanites.

Angels, as we have already seen earlier, fought for Israel, led by Deborah and Barak, against the Canaanites and their general, Sisera. *"They fought from heaven; the stars in their courses fought against Sisera"* (Judg 5:20).

Against Midianites.

The angel of the LORD assured Gideon that Israel would prevail against the Midianites. *"And the angel of the LORD appeared unto him, and said unto him, The LORD is with thee, thou mighty man of valour. And Gideon said unto him, Oh my Lord, if the LORD be with us, why then is all this befallen us? and where be all his miracles which our fathers told us of, saying, Did not the LORD bring us up from Egypt? but now the LORD hath forsaken us, and delivered us into the hands of the Midianites. And the LORD looked upon him, and said, Go in this thy might, and thou shalt save Israel from the hand of the Midianites: have not I sent thee?"* (Judg 6:12-14). Israel won.

Against Assyrians.

In the time of the prophet Elisha, the angel of the LORD himself annihilated the Assyrians who came to invade Israel. *"And when the servant of the man of God was risen early, and gone forth, behold, an host compassed the city both with horses and chariots. And his servant said unto him, Alas, my master! how shall we do? And he answered, Fear not: for they that be with us are more than they that be with them. And Elisha prayed, and said, LORD, I pray thee, open his eyes, that he may see. And the LORD opened the eyes of the young man; and he saw: and, behold, the mountain was full of horses and chariots of fire round about Elisha... And it came to pass that night, that the angel of the LORD went out, and smote in the camp of the Assyrians an hundred fourscore and five thousand: and when they arose early in the morning, behold, they were all dead corpses"* (2 Kings 6:15-17; 19:35)

Watchmen of coming dangers

When there were prophets, God warned His people through them. *"Surely the Sovereign LORD does nothing without revealing his plan to his servants the prophets"* (Amos 3:7, NIV). At other times, God informed the faithful through the angels.

Sodom and Gomorrah.

Two angels in the form of men warned Lot, Abraham's nephew, to leave Sodom with his family immediately in order to escape its imminent destruction. *"For we will destroy this place, because the cry of them is waxen great before the face of the LORD; and the LORD hath sent us to destroy it. And Lot went out, and spake unto his sons in law, which married his* daughters, and said, Up, get you out of this place; for the LORD will destroy this city. But he seemed as one that mocked unto his sons in law. And when the morning arose, then the angels hastened Lot, saying, Arise, take thy wife, and thy two daughters, which are here; lest thou be consumed in the iniquity of the city"* (Gen 19:13-15).

Slaughter of children.

The angel of the LORD instructed Joseph to bring the Christ-child and his mother to Egypt without a moment's delay to save him from the slaughter of infants ordered by Herod. *"...the angel of the Lord appeareth to Joseph in a dream, saying, Arise, and take the young child and his mother, and flee into Egypt, and be thou there until I bring thee word: for Herod will seek the young child to destroy him. When he arose, he took the young child and his mother by night, and departed into Egypt"* (Matt 2:13b-14).

End-time ordeals.

Christ sent his angel to tell John about the afflictions that will befall men in the end-times so that the faithful can prepare themselves. *"The Revelation of Jesus Christ, which God gave unto him, to shew unto his servants things which must shortly come to pass; and he sent and signified it by his angel unto his servant John"* (Rev 1:1).

Attendants of the Messiah

Angels looked after Christ, the Son of God, throughout His earthly ministry until He ascended to heaven. .

In the wilderness.

Alone by Himself, Christ fasted forty days and nights. *"And he was there in the wilderness forty days, tempted of Satan; and was with the wild beasts; and the angels ministered unto him"* (Mark 1:13).

In the garden of Gethsemane.

An angel encouraged Christ as he suffered spiritually. *"And he was withdrawn from them about a stone's cast, and kneeled down, and prayed, Saying, Father, if thou be willing, remove this cup from me: nevertheless not my will, but thine, be done. And there appeared an angel unto him from heaven, strengthening him"* (Luke 22:41-43).

At the resurrection.

It was an angel who rolled open the circular stone door of the rock-tomb where Christ had been laid to rest. *"And, behold, there was a great earthquake: for the angel of the Lord descended from heaven, and came and rolled back the stone from the door, and sat upon it. His countenance was like lightning, and his raiment white as snow: And for fear of him the keepers did shake, and became as dead men"* (Matt 28:2-4).

Mary Magdalene saw two angels inside the rock-tomb. *"But Mary stood without at the sepulchre weeping: and as she wept, she stooped down, and looked into the sepulchre, And seeth two angels in white sitting, the one at the head, and the other at the feet, where the body of Jesus had lain"* (John 20:11-12).

An angel broke the good news of Christ's resurrection. *"And the angel answered and said unto the women, Fear not ye: for I know that ye seek Jesus, which was crucified. He is not here: for he is risen, as he said. Come, see the place where the Lord lay. And go quickly, and tell his disciples that he is risen from the dead; and, behold, he goeth before you into Galilee; there shall ye see him: lo, I have told you"* (Matt 28:5-7).

At the ascension.

Forty days after the resurrection, as Christ ascended from the Mount of Olives to heaven, two angels told the disciples of Christ's future return to earth. *"And while they looked stedfastly toward heaven as he went up, behold, two men stood by them in white apparel; Which also said, Ye men of Galilee, why stand ye gazing up into heaven? this same Jesus, which is taken up from you into heaven, shall so come in like manner as ye have seen him go into heaven"* (Acts 1:10-11).

Executors of God's judgment

The LORD metes out punishment on transgressors by means of His angels, too. *"He cast upon them the fierceness of his anger, wrath, and indignation, and trouble, by sending evil angels among them"* (Ps 78:49).

David's census.

When David disobeyed the LORD by taking a census of Israel, an angel dealt the punishment upon them. *"So the LORD sent a pestilence upon Israel from the morning even to the time appointed: and there died of the people from Dan even to Beersheba seventy thousand men. And when the angel stretched out his hand upon Jerusalem to destroy it, the LORD repented him of the evil, and said to the angel that destroyed the people, It is enough: stay now thine hand"* (2 Sam 24:15-16).

Herod's arrogance.

Herod died by the hands of an angel. *"And upon a set day Herod, arrayed in royal apparel, sat upon his throne, and made an oration unto them. And the people gave a shout, saying, It is the voice of a god, and not of a man. And immediately the angel of the Lord smote him, because he gave not God the glory: and he was eaten of worms, and gave up the ghost"* (Acts 12:21-23).

Escorts to Paradise.

Angels guide the spirits of the righteous to their just heavenly rewards. In Luke 16:22, Christ tells of the angels escorting the saved to Abraham. *"And it came to pass, that the beggar died, and was carried by the angels into Abraham's bosom: the rich man also died, and was buried."*

The Great Tribulation.

At the time of the end, angels will administer the apocalyptic afflictions prophesied in the Scriptures on sinful humanity. *"And I heard a great voice out of the temple saying to the seven angels, Go your ways, and pour out the vials of the wrath of God upon the earth"* (Rev 16:1).

First resurrection or "Rapture."

At the Second Coming of Christ, it is the angels who will gather the "elect," the chosen few, dead and alive, from the farthest corners of the earth. *"And then shall appear the sign of the Son of man in heaven: and then shall all the tribes of the earth mourn, and they shall see the Son of man coming in the clouds of heaven with power and great glory. And he shall send his angels with a great sound of a trumpet, and they shall gather together his elect from the four winds, from one end of heaven to the other"* (Matt 24:30-31).

Helpers in salvation

The angels dwelling in the stars of heaven are constantly watching the affairs of all the people on earth. They rejoice at the conversion of even just one individual. *"Likewise, I say unto you, there is joy in the presence of the angels of God over one sinner that repenteth"* (Luke 15:10).

Jury of angels? It appears that on Judgment Day every man will be presented before the entire congregation of angels. *"Also I say unto you, Whosoever shall confess me before men, him shall the Son of man also confess before the angels of God: But he that denieth me before men shall be denied before the angels of God"* (Luke 12:8-9).

Round-the-clock watch?

Do angels watch us only at night, when they appear in the starry sky? On the contrary, angels watch us through all 24 hours of each day, 7 days a week. They are in the stars, and there are stars in the sky even during the day, we just cannot see them through the sun-brightened atmosphere. But, if we go inside a dark tunnel and look out, we will see stars even at noon. Or we can look down a deep well and see stars reflected in the water.

Paul probably had in mind the angels watching us when he cautioned the female worshippers. *"But every woman that prayeth or prophesieth with her head uncovered dishonoureth her head: for that is even all one as if she were shaven... For this cause ought the woman to have power on her head because of the angels"* (1 Cor 11:5,10). Comments the *International Standard Bible Encyclopaedia*: "When Paul commands the women to keep their heads covered in church because of the angels (1 Cor 11:10) he probably means that the angels, who watch all human affairs with deep interest, would be pained to see any infraction of the laws of modesty."[1]

Apostles freed from jail.

In the New Testament, we see accounts of angels coming to the rescue of embattled believers. When the high priest and the Sadducees had the apostles thrown into jail, the angel of the Lord set them free so that they could continue preaching to the people. *"Then the high priest rose up, and all they that were with him, (which is the sect of the Sadducees,) and were filled with indignation, And laid their hands on the apostles, and put them in the common prison. But the angel of the Lord by night opened the prison doors, and brought them forth, and said, Go, stand and speak in the temple to the people all the words of this life"* (Acts 5:17-20).

Evangelist led to believer.

The angel of the Lord guided the evangelist Philip, one of the seven deacons (Acts 6:5), to meet the treasurer of Ethiopia. *"And the angel of the Lord spake unto Philip, saying, Arise, and go toward the south unto the way that goeth down from Jerusalem unto Gaza, which is desert. And he arose and went: and, behold, a man of Ethiopia, an eunuch of great authority under Candace queen of the Ethiopians, who had the charge of all her treasure, and had come to Jerusalem for to worship, Was returning, and sitting in his chariot read Esaias the prophet... And Philip ran thither to him, and heard him read the prophet Esaias, and said, Understandest thou what thou readest? And he said, How can I, except some man should guide me? And he desired Philip that he would come up and sit with him... Then Philip opened his mouth, and began at the same scripture, and preached unto him Jesus. And as they went on their way, they came unto a certain water: and the eunuch said, See, here is water; what doth hinder me to be baptized? And Philip said, If thou believest with all thine heart, thou mayest. And he answered and said, I believe that Jesus Christ is the Son of God"* (Acts 8:26-28,30-31,35-37).

Centurion baptized by apostle.

It was also the angel of God who told Cornelius, a God-fearing Roman centurion, to summon Peter to his home. *"He saw in a vision evidently about the ninth hour of the day an* angel of God coming in to him, and saying unto him, Cornelius. And when he looked on him, he was afraid, and said, What is it, Lord? And he said unto him, Thy prayers and thine alms are come up for a memorial before God. And now send men to Joppa, and call for one Simon, whose surname is Peter: He lodgeth with one Simon a tanner, whose house is by the sea side: he shall tell thee what thou oughtest to do"* (Acts 10:3-6).

After hearing Peter, Cornelius and the members of his household were filled with the Holy Spirit and had themselves baptized, becoming the first Gentile converts to Christianity.

Peter's life spared.

Herod had James the brother of John put to death, then had Peter thrown into jail, intending to bring him to public trial after Passover. The angel of the Lord came on the eve of the trial. *"And when Herod would have brought him forth, the same night Peter was sleeping between two soldiers, bound with two chains: and the keepers before the door kept the prison. And, behold, the angel of the Lord came upon him, and a light shined in the prison: and he smote Peter on the side, and raised him up, saying, Arise up quickly. And his chains fell off from his hands. And the angel said unto him, Gird thyself, and bind on thy sandals. And so he did. And he saith unto him, Cast thy garment about thee, and follow me. And he went out, and followed him; and wist not that it was true which was done by the angel; but thought he saw a vision. When they were past the first and the second ward, they came unto the iron gate that leadeth unto the city; which opened to them of his own accord: and they went out, and passed on through one street; and forthwith the angel departed from him"* (Acts 12:6-10).

Paul saved at sea.

On the voyage to Rome for his trial, Paul's ship was caught in a violent storm that continued for many days. His companions began to lose hope of surviving. *"But after long abstinence Paul stood forth in the midst of them, and said, Sirs, ye should have hearkened unto me, and not have loosed from Crete, and to have gained this harm and loss. And now I exhort you to be of good cheer: for there shall be no loss of any man's life among you, but of the ship. For there stood by me this night the angel of God, whose I am, and whom I serve, Saying, Fear not, Paul; thou must be brought before Caesar: and, lo, God hath given thee all them that sail with thee. Wherefore, sirs, be of good cheer: for I believe God, that it shall be even as it was told me"* (Acts 27:21-25).

They were shipwrecked when the sailors attempted to beach the vessel, but, as the angel of God had said, none of the 276 people on board lost his life.

Prayers brought before God.

In Revelation, we are shown that the prayers of the faithful are brought by an angel with incense to the golden altar in front of God's throne. *"And another angel came and stood at the altar, having a golden censer; and there was given unto him much incense, that he should offer it with the prayers of all saints upon the golden altar which was before the throne"* (Rev 8:3). If you are one of the "saints," your prayers are highly regarded!

Guardians of the godly

The protection and assistance extended by angels to men were well known to the Israelites. The psalmist intones in Psalm 34:7 (NASU): *"The angel of the LORD encamps around those who fear Him, And rescues them."*

Today, angels who watch over people are called "guardian angels." Although the term is not found in the Bible, it is popular in our modern era and has been the subject of books, movies, television series, documentaries, and other forms of so-called infotainment. What are guardian angels supposed to do?

Psalm 91:10-13 briefly says it all: *"There shall no evil befall thee, neither shall any plague come nigh thy dwelling. For he shall give his angels charge over thee, to keep thee in all thy ways. They shall bear thee up in their hands, lest thou dash thy foot against a stone. Thou shalt tread upon the lion and adder: the young lion and the dragon shalt thou trample under feet."*

Angels protect the people they guard against all kinds of untoward incidents – they will not figure in accidents, become afflicted with dread diseases, or be attacked by wild animals. For that matter, they will not even trip on their feet!

The devil knew this and tempted Christ to demonstrate how the angels would save Him. *"Then the devil taketh him up into the holy city, and setteth him on a pinnacle of the temple, And saith unto him, If thou be the Son of God, cast thyself down: for it is written, He shall give his angels charge concerning thee: and in their hands they shall bear thee up, lest at any time thou dash thy foot against a stone"* (Matt 4:5-6).

Centuries earlier, when the king of Babylon had Daniel cast into the lions' den, the young Jewish prophet miraculously survived unscathed. *"Then said Daniel unto the king, O king, live for ever. My God hath sent his angel, and hath shut the lions' mouths, that they have not hurt me: forasmuch as before him innocency was found in me; and also before thee, O king, have I done no hurt"* (Dan 6:21-22).

Angels guard all children?

Many people today believe that all innocent little children have guardian angels. This belief is primarily based on one particular verse in the Bible. *"Take heed that ye despise not one of these little ones; for I say unto you, That in heaven their angels do always behold the face of my Father which is in heaven"* (Matt 18:10). Indeed, that is what the verse seems to say. Let us look for pertinent passages in the Scriptures.

In 2 Samuel 12:22-23a, we read about David's newborn son out of adultery with Bathsheba. *"While the child was yet alive, I fasted and wept: for I said, Who can tell whether GOD will be gracious to me, that the child may live? But now he is dead."* The infant was gravely ill, so David fasted and prayed -- to no avail; the child died just the same. It looks quite clear that, although David was beloved of God, his innocent little child had no guardian angel.

So, who were the children Christ was referring to? We find a lead to the answer in 1 Corinthians 7:14 – *"For the unbelieving husband is sanctified by the wife, and the unbelieving wife is sanctified by the husband: else were your children unclean; but now are they holy."*

Let us allow *The Wycliffe Bible Commentary* to explain: "This does not mean that a child born into a home where only one of the parents is a Christian is born 'into the family of Christ' (cf. Barclay, op. cit., p. 71). Paul simply means that the OT principle of the communication of uncleanness does not hold (cf. Hag 2:11-13). The union (marriage) is lawful and confers privilege on the members (cf. ICC, p. 142), privileges such as the protection of God…"[2]

In other words, children are made "holy," because of one faithful parent, not "unclean" owing to a faithless parent. The children are not yet spiritually saved, but they nonetheless deserve the protection of God in preparation for future salvation. Hence, they have guardian angels.

It now becomes clear that the children Christ was referring to were only the children of the disciples around Him, not all children in general. In the case of David, when his son was born, he was sinful and unclean in the sight of God.

Grownups.

Let us consider the grownup children of Job, the most pious man in his time. He prayed and made burnt offerings to God for his seven sons and three daughters, who were fond of merry-making. *"And it was so, when the days of their feasting were gone about, that Job sent and sanctified them, and rose up early in the morning, and offered burnt offerings according to the number of them all: for Job said, It may be that my sons have sinned, and cursed God in their hearts. Thus did Job continually"* (Job 1:5). Today this is called "intercessory prayer."

Yet, just like in David's case, Job's efforts came to naught. *"While he was yet speaking, there came also another, and said, Thy sons and thy daughters were eating and drinking wine in their eldest brother's house: And, behold, there came a great wind from the wilderness, and smote the four corners of the house, and it fell upon the young men, and they are dead; and I only am escaped alone to tell thee"* (Job 1:18-19).

Job's piety and intercession bore no fruit for his children. After all, they had all likely reached the age of accountability and were all answerable to God for their individual behavior.

Heirs of salvation.

So, aside from disciples' children, who are the grownups angels guard? Paul reveals the answer in Hebrews 1:13-14: *"But to which of the angels said he at any time, Sit on my right hand, until I make thine enemies thy footstool? Are they not all ministering spirits, sent forth to minister for them who shall be heirs of salvation?"*

Apparently, all of God's angels in heaven are guardians who watch over those who will inherit eternal life in the kingdom of God! Thus, if you are a future heir, you have a guardian angel and so do your innocent little children, if any. If not, you and your children have no guardian angels whatsoever and are exposed without any protection to all sorts of danger on earth.

Do you think you qualify to be a future heir of salvation, and so deserve to have a guardian angel? (We will examine the necessary qualifications in a succeeding chapter.)

Scarcer sightings

We rarely hear about contacts between angels and men in these modern times. Are angels no longer as active as before? According to *Nelson's Illustrated Bible Dictionary,* "The frequency with which angels participate in human affairs has diminished since Pentecost, probably because of the larger role played by the Holy Spirit in the lives of Christians since then."[3]

These days, we receive messages from God not through angels, but through the Holy Spirit. *"But God hath revealed them unto us by his Spirit: for the Spirit searcheth all things, yea, the deep things of God"* (1 Cor 2:10).

3

Rebels and Renegades

Behold, he put no trust in his servants; and his angels he charged with folly...

-- Job 4:18.

The angels God created are not all the same. Although most single-mindedly serve the LORD, each angel is individually unique, with his own mind, personality and temperament.

A very special angel

One angel is said to have been the epitome of intelligence and good looks – the picture of perfection! *"Thus saith the Lord GOD; Thou sealest up the sum, full of wisdom, and perfect in beauty... Thou wast perfect in thy ways from the day that thou wast created, till iniquity was found in thee"* (Ezek 28:12,15).

The prophet was referring to Lucifer. *"How art thou fallen from heaven, O Lucifer, son of the morning! how art thou cut down to the ground, which didst weaken the nations!"* (Isa 14:12). In the entire Bible, the name "Lucifer" occurs in this verse only. We have learned earlier that "Lucifer" in Latin means "light-bearer." It has been derived from the Hebrew word *helel,* which translates in English as "the shining one."

In the Hebrew text of Genesis 2:4, the letter *hey,* the initial of *helel*, appears smaller than the other letters. Was this a sign that Lucifer had been minimized in the sight of the all-knowing Creator from the very beginning?

Morning stars

The "morning stars" are a very special kind of angels. In the King James Version (KJV) of the Bible (1611), Christ refers to Himself as the "morning star." *"I Jesus have sent mine angel to testify unto you these things in the churches. I am the root and the offspring of David, and the bright and morning star"* (Rev 22:16).

Many new Bible students are surprised to learn that there are more than one morning star besides the Son of God. We have noted in Job 38:7 -- *"the morning stars sang together, and all the sons of God shouted for joy..."*

Oddly, the more recent New International Version (NIV, 1978) translation calls both Christ and Lucifer "morning star."

Lucifer in Isaiah 14:12 (NIV) -- *"How you have fallen from heaven, O morning star, son of the dawn! You have been cast down to the earth, you who once laid low the nations!"*

Christ in Revelation 22:16 (NIV) -- *"I, Jesus, have sent my angel to give you this testimony for the churches. I am the Root and the Offspring of David, and the bright Morning Star."*

In 2 Peter 1:19 (NIV), we see another morning star! *"And we have the word of the prophets made more certain, and you will do well to pay attention to it, as to a light shining in a dark place, until the day dawns and the morning star rises in your hearts."*

Matthew Henry's Commentary identifies this "morning star": "When the light of the scripture is darted into the blind mind and dark understanding by the Holy Spirit of God, then the spiritual day dawns and the day-star arises in that soul. This enlightening of a dark benighted mind is like the day-break that improves and advances, spreads and diffuses itself through the whole soul, till it makes perfect day, Prov 4:18."[1] It is the "light of the scripture."

A "cherub that covers"

One epithet for Lucifer that is often glossed over as too mysterious, but of minor importance, is in Ezekiel 28:14,16 --

"Thou art the anointed cherub that covereth; and I have set thee so: thou wast upon the holy mountain of God; thou hast walked up and down in the midst of the stones of fire... By the multitude of thy merchandise they have filled the midst of thee with violence, and thou hast sinned: therefore I will cast thee as profane out of the mountain of God: and I will destroy thee, O covering cherub, from the midst of the stones of fire"

The verse speaks of Lucifer as the "cherub that covers" and "covering cherub." What did he cover? Bible commentaries are at a loss. Let us do some scriptural digging ourselves.

Patterns in heaven.

All the things God told Moses to make – from the tabernacle to the furniture and utensils to be used with it – were all patterned after originals that God had shown him. *"And let them make me a sanctuary; that I may dwell among them. According to all that I shew thee, after the pattern of the tabernacle, and the pattern of all the instruments thereof, even so shall ye make it... And look that thou make them after their pattern, which was shewed thee in the mount"* (Ex 25:8-9,40).

Paul corroborates: *"They serve at a sanctuary that is a copy and shadow of what is in heaven. This is why Moses was warned when he was about to build the tabernacle: "See to it that you make everything according to the pattern shown you on the mountain'"* (Heb 8:5-6, NIV). The tabernacle (Tent of Meeting) in the wilderness (later replaced by the Temple in Jerusalem) and its furniture were all copies of heavenly originals!

Temple. There is a temple of the tabernacle in heaven (*"the temple of the tabernacle of the testimony in heaven was opened"* -- Rev 15:5);

Altar of incense. This holy fixture (Ex 30:27, 31:8) has a counterpart in heaven (*"another angel came and stood at the altar, having a golden censer; and there was given unto him much incense, that he should offer it with the prayers of all saints upon the golden altar which was before the throne"* -- Rev 8:3).

Lamp-stand. The seven-branched *Menorah* (Ex 25:31-39) in the earthly Tabernacle had a heavenly prototype (*"there were seven lamps of fire burning before the throne, which are the seven Spirits of God"* -- Rev 4:5).

Ark of the covenant. Also called "ark of testament" or "ark of testimony" (Ex 25:10-22), it is an earthly facsimile of the heavenly (*"the temple of God was opened in heaven, and there was seen in his temple the ark of his testament"* -- Rev 11:19).

"Mercy seat." The ark or chest had a lid or covering called "mercy seat." *"And they shall make an ark of shittim wood: two cubits and a half shall be the length thereof, and a cubit and a half the breadth thereof, and a cubit and a half the height thereof... And thou shalt make a mercy seat of pure gold: two cubits and a half shall be the length thereof, and a cubit and a half the breadth thereof"* (Ex 25:10,17).

Fausset's Bible Dictionary emphasizes: "The mercy seat was never simply called "the cover" of the ark, but had a separate importance of its own. The holy of holies is called '*the place of the mercy-seat*' (1 Chron 28:11; Lev 16:2), showing that it was not a mere part of the ark."[2]

Why was it called a "seat"? Who was supposed to sit on it?" Here is a clue. *"And the LORD said unto Moses, Speak unto Aaron thy brother, that he come not at all times into the holy place within the vail before the mercy seat, which is upon the ark; that he die not: for I will appear in the cloud upon the mercy seat"* (Lev 16:2).

Nelson's Illustrated Bible Dictionary gets straight to the point. "The golden lid or covering on the ARK OF THE COVENANT, regarded as the resting place of God (Ex 25:17-22; 1 Chron 28:11; Heb 9:5)..."[3] The mercy seat was where God rested, the place where He sat; it was therefore His throne on earth!

Sometime later, the LORD told Moses that Aaron should sprinkle the blood of sacrificed goats and bullocks upon and before the mercy seat (Lev 16:14-15). The blood, which atoned for the soul (Lev 17:11), was to be offered to God on the mercy seat, His throne on earth, from which He showed mercy and forgave the sins of the people.

Cherubs above. Moses was told to fashion two golden cherubs on top of the mercy seat, *"And thou shalt make two cherubims of gold, of beaten work shalt thou make them, in the two ends of the mercy seat... And the cherubims shall stretch forth their wings on high, covering the mercy seat with their wings, and their faces shall look one to another; toward the* *mercy seat shall the faces of the cherubims be. And thou shalt put the mercy seat above upon the ark..."* (Ex 25:18,20-21a).

The psalmist sings in Psalm 99:1 (NIV) -- *"The LORD reigns, let the nations tremble; he sits enthroned between the cherubim, let the earth shake."* God is sitting on a throne that is between cherubs. Get the picture?

If the mercy seat covered by the wings of two golden cherubs was the throne of God on earth representing His throne in heaven, then God's celestial throne must have also been covered by the wings of two cherubim – "two cherubs that cover"! Was Lucifer one of them? Who was the other one?

Ambitious angel

Presumably due to his extraordinary endowments, Lucifer's ego swelled. *"Thine heart was lifted up because of thy beauty, thou hast corrupted thy wisdom by reason of thy brightness..."* (Ezek 28:17a). He desired to rise above all other angels; he even wanted to become like God! *"For thou hast said in thine heart, I will ascend into heaven, I will exalt my throne above the stars of God: I will sit also upon the mount of the congregation, in the sides of the north: I will ascend above the heights of the clouds; I will be like the most High"* (Isa 14:13-14).

A murderer since creation.

Christ, telling the Jews how wicked they had become, figuratively said their father was Satan, who had been a killer from the time he was created. *"Ye are of your father the devil, and the lusts of your father ye will do. He was a murderer from the beginning"* (John 8:44). Several instances in Scriptures illustrate why this is so.

"Eat your vegetables." After the creation, God gave man, all the land animals, birds, and reptiles the green plants on earth for food. *"And to every beast of the earth, and to every fowl of the air, and to every thing that creepeth upon the earth, wherein there is life, I have given every green herb for meat: and it was so"* (Gen 1:30). In modern terms, the first men and animals on dry land were all what we call today "vegetarians."

Here we see God's marvelous wisdom. Man and animals need nutrients from the earth for growth and good health. Adam did not eat soil, so he and the animals got the nutrients in a second-hand manner -- by eating plant food in the form of vegetables and fruits full of nutrients from the earth. The largest creatures in the prehistoric world were herbivores – the plant-eating dinosaurs. Titanosaurus stood some 65 feet tall (as high as a 7-story building), was 130 feet long, and weighed 77 tons! Tyrannosaurus Rex tipped the scales at only 7 tons.

Today, when we eat animal products, we get the nutrients third-hand, having passed through plants first and animals next.

Sometime in prehistory, some animals began eating other animals. What happened? How did the carnivores, the meat-eating animals, arise in disobedience to God's command?

Violent devil. The prophet Ezekiel tells of a violent streak having arisen in Satan. *"By the multitude of thy merchandise they have filled the midst of thee with violence, and thou hast sinned: therefore I will cast thee as profane out of the mountain of God: and I will destroy thee, O covering cherub, from the midst of the stones of fire"* (Ezek 28:16).

Author Dennis Petersen muses: "Some suggest that Satan created some of the grotesque giants of the prehistoric past... is he the one ultimately responsible for the perversion of life? Does the Bible say anything about a demonically linked corruption of Earth's animal life?"[4]

Did Satan incite the plant-eating animals to fight each other, then induced the stronger victors to eat the fallen victims?

Fired out watcher?

We discovered in Chapter 1 that four kinds of creature God created on the fifth and sixth days of creation ("fowl," "beast of the earth," "cattle," and man) have angelic watchers with faces resembling theirs ("eagle," "lion," "calf," and "man"). Incidentally, all four are warm-blooded land creatures.

Cold-blooded creatures. Two other kinds -- water creatures and creeping things -- are mostly cold-blooded. We earlier read the prophet Habakkuk saying that these last two kinds have no watchers over them. *"And makest men as the fishes of the sea, as the creeping things, that have no ruler over them?"* (Hab 1:14). (The watchers who look after the welfare of the creatures under them are also called "rulers.")

In the Revelation, we see two physical forms that Satan can appear in: *"And the great dragon was cast out, that old serpent, called the Devil, and Satan, which deceiveth the whole world: he was cast out into the earth, and his angels were cast out with him"* (Rev 12:9). "Dragon" and "serpent" are both cold-blooded reptiles, which are creeping things.

Was their look-alike Satan their former ruler? Was Satan fired out of his job as watcher over creeping things because he incited them to kill and devour one another?

A plotter in Paradise

We learn from Ezekiel that Lucifer was in the garden of Eden. *"Thou hast been in Eden the garden of God; every precious stone was thy covering, the sardius, topaz, and the diamond, the beryl, the onyx, and the jasper, the sapphire, the emerald, and the carbuncle, and gold: the workmanship of thy tabrets and of thy pipes was prepared in thee in the day that thou wast created"* (Ezek 28:13).

The Garden was created before Adam, so it is possible that the devil or serpent was already there when the LORD placed the Adam in the garden.

Satan might have felt jealous when the Creator made man the master of all living things that move on earth. *"And God said, Let us make man in our image, after our likeness: and let them have dominion over the fish of the sea, and over the fowl of the air, and over the cattle, and over all the earth, and over every creeping thing that creepeth upon the earth… And God blessed them, and God said unto them, Be fruitful, and multiply, and replenish the earth, and subdue it: and have dominion over the fish of the sea, and over the fowl of the air, and over every living thing that moveth upon the earth"* (Gen 1:26,28).

Scheme to kill Adam.

Satan must have wanted the earth for himself. He might have overheard God and knew Adam would die if the man disobeyed God and partook of the fruit of the forbidden tree. Satan caused Adam to sin through his young partner Eve.

Satan was probably very much puzzled and disappointed when Adam did not die immediately. (Adam would eventually die at the age of 930 years much later.) Nevertheless, Satan must have gloated with glee when Adam and Eve were driven out of the Garden of Eden.

The power of death

Satan acquired the power of death. We read in Hebrews 2:14 -- *"Forasmuch then as the children are partakers of flesh and blood, he also himself likewise took part of the same; that through death he might destroy him that had the power of death, that is, the devil."*

Fausset's Bible Dictionary remarks: "Satan has 'the power of death,' because 'the sting of death is sin' (1 Cor 15:56); Satan being the author of sin is also the author of its consequence, death."[5] Two apostles explain further. John in 1 John 3:4 (*"Whosoever committeth sin transgresseth also the law: for sin is the transgression of the law."*); and Paul in Romans 6:23a (*"For the wages of sin is death."*). In short, when Satan causes someone to break any of God's instructions, that person sins and will have to die as a consequence.

A habit and a hobby.

It looks like killing became a habit, maybe even a hobby, with Satan. The following are some of the well known Biblical instances when he committed or attempted murder..

Abel. Satan evidently induced Cain to kill his brother Abel, as suggested by the circumstances. *"Do not be like Cain, who belonged to the evil one and murdered his brother. And why did he murder him? Because his own actions were evil and his brother's were righteous"* (1 John 3:12-13, NIV).

Job. God knew Satan wanted to kill Job and so warned him against it. *"So the LORD said to Satan, "Behold, all that he has is in your power; only do not lay a hand on his person..."* (Job 1:12a, NKJV).

Christ. At the Messiah's birth, *"the dragon stood before the woman which was ready to be delivered, for to devour her child as soon as it was born"* (Rev 12:4b). In the attempt to kill the Christ-child, Satan used King Herod to order the massacre of all children below two years of age in Bethlehem. *"Then Herod, when he saw that he was mocked of the wise men, was* *exceeding wroth, and sent forth, and slew all the children that were in Bethlehem, and in all the coasts thereof, from two years old and under, according to the time which he had diligently inquired of the wise men"* (Matt 2:16).

Over three decades later, Satan succeeded in having Christ crucified, but did not know that the Messiah would become even more powerful in death. *"But we speak the wisdom of God in a mystery, even the hidden wisdom, which God ordained before the world unto our glory: Which none of the princes of this world knew: for had they known it, they would not have crucified the Lord of glory."*

Pseudonyms and aliases

The evil one has no real name, and just like some inveterate criminals today, he goes by many pseudonyms and aliases.

Lucifer. As we have already seen, this s a Latin term that means "light-bearer," derived from the Hebrew word *helel*, translated in English as "the shining one."

Satan. Not a name, but a sobriquet, English short form of the Greek *Satanas*, which means "adversary" or "opponent." *Nelson's Illustrated Bible Dictionary* notes: "Since his fall, Satan has opposed God's plan to establish His kingdom on earth. He tricked Eve (Gen 3:1-5) in order to use man to establish his kingdom rather than God's. Satan later opposed Jesus by questioning His identity as the Messiah and by tempting Him to misuse His powers as God's Son (Matt 4:1-11)."[6]

Devil. English transliteration of the Greek *diabolos*, which means "slanderer" or "false accuser." In Revelation 12:10b, John calls him *"the accuser of our brethren... which accused them before our God day and night."*

In Genesis 3:2-4, the devil insinuated to Eve that God was a liar. Eve said, *"But of the fruit of the tree which is in the midst of the garden, God hath said, Ye shall not eat of it, neither shall ye touch it, lest ye die. And the serpent said unto the woman, Ye shall not surely die."* In Job 1:10b-11 (NIV), the devil maligned Job to God. *"You have blessed the work of his hands, so that his flocks and herds are spread throughout the land. But stretch out your hand and strike everything he has, and he will surely curse you to your face."*

The word "devils" in the KJV is a vocabulary slip. There is only one "devil" – Satan. His minions are the "demons," a word not found in the KJV, where they are called "unclean spirits."

Dragon. Expounds *Fausset's Bible Dictionary*: "In the New Testament it symbolizes Satan the old serpent (Gen 3), combining gigantic strength with craft, malignity, and venom (Rev 12:3). The dragon's color, 'red,' fiery red, implies that he was a murderer from the beginning."[7]

Serpent. The *International Standard Bible Encyclopaedia* notes: "Most of the Biblical references to serpents are of a figurative nature, and they usually imply poisonous qualities. The wicked (Ps 58:4), the persecutor (Ps 140:3), and the enemy (Jer 8:17) are likened to venomous serpents."[8]

Beelzebub/Beelzebul. *Nelson's Illustrated Bible Dictionary* explains: "Baal-Zebub, which means "lord of the fly," was "the god of Ekron" (2 Kings 1:2-3,6,16)... This god was worshiped as the producer of flies, and consequently as the god that was able to defend against this pest."[9] *Fausset's Bible Dictionary* adds: "The Jews, in ridicule, changed Baal-zebub, the Ekronite god of flies, into Beelzebul, 'god of dung'."[10]

Belial. The *International Standard Bible Encyclopaedia* states that "'Belial; became a proper name for Satan, or for Antichrist (thus frequently in the Jewish Apocalyptic writings, e.g. in XII P, Book Jub, Asc Isa, Sib Or). In this sense Paul used the word in 2 Cor 6:15,"[11] *"And what concord hath Christ with Belial? or what part hath he that believeth with an infidel?"*

The pseudonym comes from *beli* ("without") and *ya'al* ("usefulness"), i.e., good-for-nothing. A "man of Belial" is a worthless, lawless fellow[12] (Deut 13:13; Judg 19:22; 1 Sam 2:12). Indeed, the name is a fitting one for him who has nothing to offer men but trouble and ruin.

Azazel (scapegoat). On the Day of Atonement (Lev 16:8-10), the high priest cast lots upon two goats -- "one lot for the LORD, and the other lot for Azazel."[13] The first was presented as a sin-offering to God; the other (the "scapegoat") symbolically received the sins of the people and was then driven into the wilderness over a precipice to its death. According to *The New Unger's Bible Dictionary,* "Many believe Azazel to be a personal being, either a spirit, a demon, or Satan himself."[14]

Abaddon or Apollyon. These two names are seen only in Revelation 9:11 (*"And they had a king over them, which is the angel of the bottomless pit, whose name in the Hebrew tongue is Abaddon, but in the Greek tongue hath his name Apollyon"*), Abaddon means "destruction" in Hebrew; while Apollyon signifies "destroyer" in Greek.

Deceiver. Of Revelation 20:10, *Nelson's Illustrated Bible Dictionary*, says, "Starting with Eve, the devil has attempted to deceive every living soul. Evil men operating under the power of the evil one will continue to deceive (2 Tim 3:13)."[15] Moreover, the Bible tells us in John 8:44 -- *"Ye are of your father the devil, and the lusts of your father ye will do. He was a murderer from the beginning, and abode not in the truth, because there is no truth in him. When he speaketh a lie, he speaketh of his own: for he is a liar, and the father of it."* As supreme deceiver, Satan is the father of lies and liars.

Prince of this world. It looks like Satan's ambition has taken him places. He is today the "prince of this world." Christ called him so several times. *"Hereafter I will not talk much with you: for the prince of this world cometh, and hath nothing in me"* (John 14:30; cf. vv. 12:31, 16:11).

Here, "prince" does not mean son of the king. *Nelson's Illustrated Bible Dictionary* points out, "A leader or ruler. The common elements in the many different words translated as prince in the Bible are leadership and authority. The word often denotes royalty, but it just as frequently describes leadership in general. Both Abraham (Gen 23:6) and Solomon (1 Kings 11:34) were called princes. Tribal leaders of early Israel were often designated as princes."[16]

But, we wonder, why is Satan called "prince" or ruler? *Matthew Henry's Commentary on the Whole Bible: New Modern Edition* observes that: "It is the devil that is here called the prince of this world, because he rules over the men of the world by the things of the world…"[17]

God of this world. This sobriquet is both surprising and unnerving. *"In whom the god of this world hath blinded the minds of them which believe not, lest the light of the glorious gospel of Christ, who is the image of God, should shine unto them"* (2 Cor 4:4). According to *Barnes' Notes*, "2 Cor 4:4; Eph

6:12: The rulers of the darkness of this world -- that is, the rulers of this dark world, a well-known Hebraism... All these names are given him from the influence or power which he has over the men of this world, because the great mass of men have been under his control and subject to his will."[18]

Matthew Henry adds: "The god of this world hath blinded their minds, v. 4. They are under the influence and power of the devil, who is here called the god of this world, and elsewhere the prince of this world, because of... the great sway that, by divine permission, he bears in the world... And as he is the prince of darkness, and ruler of the darkness of this world, so he darkens the understandings of men, and increases their prejudices, and supports his interest by keeping them in the dark, blinding their minds with ignorance, and error, and prejudices, that they should not behold the light of the glorious gospel of Christ..."[19]

Thus, he "has dominion over the world. They obey his will; they execute his plans; they further his purposes, and they are his obedient subjects. He has subdued the world to himself, and was really adored in the place of the true God; see the note on 1 Cor 10:20. 'They sacrificed to devils and not to God.'"[20]

Prince of the power of the air. This epithet is intriguing. *"Wherein in time past ye walked according to the course of this world, according to the prince of the power of the air, the spirit that now worketh in the children of disobedience"* (Eph 2:2).

Barnes' Notes comments: "Doddridge supposes that it means that he controls the fallen spirits who are permitted to range the regions of the atmosphere... The opinion may have been either that such spirits 'dwelt' in the air, or that they had control over it, according to the later Jewish belief... And who can tell what control may have been given to such fallen spirits over the regions of the atmosphere -- over clouds, and storms, and pestilential air?"[21]

As "prince of the power of the air," Satan might have been responsible for several unsettling incidents in the Bible.

<u>Whirlwind killed Job's children.</u> *"While he was yet speaking, there came also another, and said, Thy sons and thy daughters were eating and drinking wine in their eldest brother's house: And, behold, there came a great wind from the wilderness, and smote the four corners of the house, and it fell upon the young*

men, and they are dead; and I only am escaped alone to tell thee" (Job 1:18-19). Unable to kill Job, Satan killed his children.

Christ's boat caught in a tempest. *"And, behold, there arose a great tempest in the sea, insomuch that the ship was covered with the waves: but he was asleep. And his disciples came to him, and awoke him, saying, Lord, save us: we perish. And he saith unto them, Why are ye fearful, O ye of little faith? Then he arose, and rebuked the winds and the sea; and there was a great calm"* (Matt 8:24-26). Could it be that Satan himself spawned the tempest, and it was him whom Christ rebuked?

Storm shipwrecked Paul. Paul almost died at sea on his way to Rome. *"When neither sun nor stars appeared for many days and the storm continued raging, we finally gave up all hope of being saved"* (Acts 27:20, NIV). Paul, however, survived.

Lightning, electricity, airwaves. Some Bible teachers say that the "power of the air" includes lightning, which is a form of electricity. If so, then it was also Satan who caused Job's financial ruin. *"While he was yet speaking, there came also another, and said, The fire of God is fallen from heaven, and hath burned up the sheep, and the servants, and consumed them; and I only am escaped alone to tell thee"* (Job 1:16).

Even radio and television airwaves, computer and internet cyberspace, may be under the power of Satan today.

Planet Earth's overseer? *Fausset's Bible Dictionary* notes that Satan "had some special connection, possibly as God's vicegerent over this earth and the animal kingdom; thereby we can understand his connection and that of his subordinate fallen angels with this earth throughout Scripture, commencing with his temptation of man..."[22]

It seems Satan had been the overseer of the earth for a long time. He appeared to have made regular reports to God on the condition of the planet. *"Now there was a day when the sons of God came to present themselves before the LORD, and Satan came also among them. And the LORD said unto Satan, Whence comest thou? Then Satan answered the LORD, and said, From going to and fro in the earth, and from walking up and down in it"* (Job 1:6-7).

Satan told Christ that power over the kingdoms of the world had been given to him. *"And the devil said unto him, All this* power will I give thee, and the glory of them: for that is delivered unto me; and to whomsoever I will I give it". (Luke 4:6). If that is true, this is one rare instance that Satan told the truth!

Goat-demons

Satan has taken on a hairy form. We gather from Psalm 68:21 -- *"But God shall wound the head of his enemies, and the hairy scalp of such an one as goeth on still in his trespasses."*

The verse implies that Satan has become hairy and keeps on violating God's will. "Hairy" in Hebrew is *sear*, which comes from *saar*, also the root-word of *sair*, meaning "devil, goat, satyr." In Bible translations, "the King James Version has 'devils,' the Revised Version (British and American) 'he-goats,' the English Revised Version margin 'satyrs'."[23]

Satan and his demons have taken on the form of he-goats. *"They shall no longer sacrifice their sacrifices to the goat demons with which they play the harlot"* (Lev 17:7a, NASU). They were worshipped as such by kings who built altars to them. *"He set up priests of his own for the high places, for the satyrs and for the calves which he had made"* (2 Chron 11:15, NASU)

At the Last Judgment, those who will be condemned to eternal damnation are compared to goats. *"When the Son of man shall come in his glory, and all the holy angels with him, then shall he sit upon the throne of his glory: And before him shall be gathered all nations: and he shall separate them one from another, as a shepherd divideth his sheep from the goats: And he shall set the sheep on his right hand, but the goats on the left"* (Matt 25:31-33). At the end of the day, it turns out that Satan, the black sheep of the family... is a goat!

The first transgender?

Some preachers say Satan is a woman. Others go so far as to claim that God created Satan to be His wife. They point to the jewelry that Satan used to wear – *"Thou hast been in Eden the garden of God; every precious stone was thy covering, the sardius, topaz, and the diamond, the beryl, the onyx, and the jasper, the sapphire, the emerald, and the carbuncle, and gold: the workmanship of thy tabrets and of thy pipes was prepared in thee in the day that thou wast created"* (Ezek 28:13).

Ashtoreth. Apostate Israelites venerated the devil as, surprise!, a goddess. *"Because that they have forsaken me, and have worshipped Ashtoreth the goddess of the Zidonians..."* (1 Kings 11:33). The gender of the deity Ashtoreth was ambiguous. "The name and cult of the goddess were derived from Babylonia, where Istar represented the evening and morning stars and was accordingly androgynous in origin. Under Semitic influence, however, she became solely female, but retained a memory of her primitive character by standing, alone among the Assyro-Bab goddesses, on a footing of equality with the male divinities. From Babylonia the worship of the goddess was carried to the Semites of the West, and in most instances the feminine suffix was attached to her name; where this was not the case the deity was regarded as a male."[24] Note that Ashtoreth (plural *Ashtaroth*) was also a morning star.

Queen of heaven.

"Ashtoreth was called 'the queen of heaven' the wife of Baal or Moloch, 'king of heaven.'"[25] *"And they forsook the LORD, and served Baal and Ashtaroth"* (Judg 2:13).

Astarte, Inanna, Ishtar, Aphrodite, Venus. The goddess had several names in the ancient world. "The Ashtaroth were worshiped by other peoples under such names as Astarte (Phoenicians and Canaanites), Inanna (Sumerians), Ishtar (Babylonians), Aphrodite (Greeks), and Venus (Romans)."[26] The name of the goddess Ishtar gave birth to the word Easter.

Venus is the evening star, the first to appear and brightest star in the evening, while the morning star is the last star to fade out at dawn – which is also Venus! It was the star known in Hebrew as *helel*, "the shining one" – Lucifer!

Worldly angels

Some angels, turning their backs on God, committed sin. Job's friend Eliphaz knew it. *"Behold, he put no trust in his servants; and his angels he charged with folly"* (Job 4:18-19).

A number of angels left their home-stars and came down to earth to take wives. *"And it came to pass, when men began to multiply on the face of the earth, and daughters were born unto them, That the sons of God saw the daughters of men that they* were fair; and they took them wives of all which they chose" (Gen 6:1-2). The truant angels were not content to have just one wife each. They took all the women they fancied, thus probably introducing polygamy in the ancient world.

Angels changing forms.

Angels are non-physical spirits, how could they have had sexual intercourse with physical humans? We get a hint from Psalm 68:17 -- *"The chariots of God are twenty thousand, even thousands of angels: the Lord is among them, as in Sinai, in the holy place."* In this verse, the Hebrew word used for "angels" is *shin'an*, from the root-word *shana*, which means to alter or change – a clue that angels can alter or change their forms.

As we discussed in Chapter 1, spirit is a form of energy; which, as high school physics teaches, can transform into matter according to Albert Einstein's famous equation $E = mc^2$. What is more, physicists theorize that all matter and energy are made up of the same basic element; but appear in different forms – e.g., air, water, wood, stone, metal – as a result of the varying vibrations of their atoms. A simple example is water, which is liquid when its atoms are vibrating moderately. When the atoms are made to vibrate much slower by freezing, it becomes solid ice. And when the atoms are caused to vibrate rapidly by heating, it turns to gaseous steam.

Did the renegade angels who came down to earth to take wives have the ability to alter the vibrations of their atoms and thus change from spirit and light into flesh and blood?

Physical sensations. Incarnate angels seem to experience the same physical sensations as men. Look at how Abraham entertained angels who visited him. *"Let a little water, I pray you, be fetched, and wash your feet, and rest yourselves under the tree: And I will fetch a morsel of bread, and comfort ye your hearts; after that ye shall pass on: for therefore are ye come to your servant. And they said, So do, as thou hast said. And Abraham hastened into the tent unto Sarah, and said, Make ready quickly three measures of fine meal, knead it, and make cakes upon the hearth. And Abraham ran unto the herd, and fetcht a calf tender and good, and gave it unto a young man; and he hasted to dress it. And he took butter, and milk, and the* *calf which he had dressed, and set it before them; and he stood by them under the tree, and they did eat"* (Gen 18:4-8). The angels must have felt thirst, fatigue, hunger, and the heat of the sun, so they ate, and under the shade of a tree. Similarly, the renegade angels must have experienced sexual pleasure, too.

Giant offspring.
The union of angels and mortal women produced gigantic children. *"There were giants in the earth in those days; and also after that, when the sons of God came in unto the daughters of men, and they bare children to them, the same became mighty men which were of old, men of renown"* (Gen 6:4).

Gigantic gays? Their appetite for sex seemingly insatiable, some fallen angels appear to have even become homosexuals. *"And the angels which kept not their first estate, but left their own habitation, he hath reserved in everlasting chains under darkness unto the judgment of the great day. Even as Sodom and Gomorrha, and the cities about them in like manner, giving themselves over to fornication, and going after strange flesh, are set forth for an example, suffering the vengeance of eternal fire"* (Jude 6-7). Their comparison to Sodom and Gomorrah seemingly alludes to the similarity of their sexual immorality and perversions.

Barnes' Notes explains the phrase "going after strange flesh": "Margin: 'other.' The reference seems to be to the unusual sin which, from the name Sodom, has been called 'sodomy.' Compare Rom 1:27. The meaning of the phrase 'going after' is, that they were greatly addicted to this vice. The word 'strange, or other,' refers to that which is contrary to nature."[27]

Imprisoned in Tartarus.
Before too long, however, the renegade angels were rounded up and imprisoned. *"And the angels who did not keep their proper domain, but left their own abode, He has reserved in everlasting chains under darkness for the judgment of the great day"* (Jude 6, NKJV). They had been chained in a place of darkness to await final sentencing.

"For if God spared not the angels that sinned, but cast them down to hell, and delivered them into chains of darkness, to be

reserved unto judgment" (2 Peter 2:4). The word translated "hell" in English is *Tartarus* in the original Greek text -- a dark pit that in Greek mythology is as far below the surface of the earth as heaven is above the earth. That sounds like a black hole deep in the core of planet Earth!

Repentant angels?

After the crucifixion, Christ visited spirits in prison before rising from the dead,. *"By which also he went and preached unto the spirits in prison; Which sometime were disobedient"* (1 Peter 3:19-20b). The disobedient spirits in prison Christ preached to sound like the fallen angels who had come down to earth to take mortal wives.

And it looks like they repented! Psalm 68:18 says, *"Thou hast ascended on high, thou hast led captivity captive: thou hast received gifts for men; yea, for the rebellious also, that the LORD God might dwell among them."* The thought is repeated in Ephesians 4:7-8 (NAS), *"But to each one of us grace was given according to the measure of Christ's gift. Therefore it says, 'When He ascended on high, He led captive a host of captives, And He gave gifts to men'."* The passages seem to say that the renegade angels repented of their sin and were forgiven through grace in Christ, who had received the power to forgive sins as a gift from the Almighty Father.

To paraphrase: From being captives of sin, the fallen angels became captives of Christ. Does the phrase *"that the LORD God might dwell among them"* mean that Christ took them back with Him to heavenly places?

Barnes' Notes comments: "As applied in the Christian sense, this would refer to those who were captives to Satan, and who were held in bondage by him, but who had been rescued by the Redeemer, and brought under another captivity -- the yielding of voluntary service to himself. Those once captives to sin were now led by him, captives in a higher sense."[28] The verses therefore can also be interpreted to mean sinners in general, both angels and men.

4

Battleground Earth!

Woe to the inhabiters of the earth and of the sea! for the devil is come down unto you, having great wrath...

-- Revelation 12:12b.

Few men realize it, but all people on earth are in the crosshairs of a raging war – a clash between unseen spiritual forces. We learn from the Bible where the conflict began – in heaven.

Vision in heaven

First, a vision materialized in the sky. *"And there appeared a great wonder in heaven; a woman clothed with the sun, and the moon under her feet, and upon her head a crown of twelve stars"* (Rev 12:1). The verse is from the book of Revelation and, as such, is full of prophetic symbols. Thank God, the keys and clues to symbols are also in the Bible. The Bible interprets itself!

A woman in prophecy, as we have seen earlier, personifies a faith, church, or religion. For example, the "virgin daughter of Zion" and "daughter of Jerusalem" in Lamentations 2:13 are a metaphor for a pure, righteous faith or religion. On the other hand, the "whore" or "harlot" spoken about in Revelation 17:1, 15-16 signifies a sinful church or religion.

We get the meaning of "clothed with the sun" in the "sun of righteousness" of Malachi 4:2. The "moon under her feet" refers to the pagan goddess symbolized by the moon and worshipped as the queen of heaven in Jeremiah 7:18. The "twelve stars" in her crown point to the sons of Jacob in Joseph's dream (Gen 37:9) who fathered the twelve tribes of Israel.

Therefore, the "woman clothed with the sun" symbolizes the pure, holy faith of the Hebrew nation – Zion -- which began with the covenant between God and Abraham, the first Hebrew.

Advent and ascent of Christ.

The "woman" (Zion) gave birth to a male infant. *"And she brought forth a man child, who was to rule all nations with a rod of iron: and her child was caught up unto God, and to his throne"* (Rev 12:5). The "*man child*" was the Messiah. The phrase "*caught up unto God*" means Christ ascended to heaven to take His place at the right hand of God (Mark 16:19, etc.).

"And the woman fled into the wilderness, where she hath a place prepared of God, that they should feed her there a thousand two hundred and threescore days" (Rev 12:6). The fledgling Christian church had to escape persecution after the Crucifixion and destruction of Jerusalem by the Romans in 70 AD. The early Christians were dispersed ("*the woman fled*") to many places in Europe, Africa, and Asia ("*into the wilderness*").

Hostilities broke out in the celestial realms. *"And there was war in heaven: Michael and his angels fought against the dragon; and the dragon fought and his angels"* (Rev 12:7). We are not told in the book of Revelation what sparked the conflict. However, we find the reason in an earlier, thinly veiled prophecy in the book of the prophet Zechariah.

The usurper.

Zechariah 3:1 reads: *"And he shewed me Joshua the high priest standing before the angel of the LORD, and Satan standing at his right hand to resist him."* In the prophetic text, Joshua embodies Christ Himself. (The names "Joshua" and "Jesus" both came from the same original – "Yahushua" – so Joshua clearly means Christ in the prophecy.) The "angel of the LORD" represents God.

Thus, when Christ arrived in heaven, He found that Satan had already positioned himself at the right hand of the angel of the LORD (representing God) before He came! Satan had usurped His place. This precipitated the war in heaven.

"Now Joshua was clothed with filthy garments, and stood before the angel. And he answered and spake unto those that stood before him, saying, Take away the filthy garments from him. And unto him he said, Behold, I have caused thine iniquity to pass from thee, and I will clothe thee with change of raiment" (Zech 3:3-4). The "filthy garments" stood for the sins of mankind that Christ had taken upon Himself. The "change of raiment" means He was made pure again in the sight of God.

Losers cast out

Satan and his hordes were defeated. *"And prevailed not; neither was their place found any more in heaven. And the great dragon was cast out, that old serpent, called the Devil, and Satan, which deceiveth the whole world: he was cast out into the earth, and his angels were cast out with him" "* (Rev 12:8-9).

They are now here! *"Therefore rejoice, ye heavens, and ye that dwell in them. Woe to the inhabiters of the earth and of the sea! for the devil is come down unto you, having great wrath, because he knoweth that he hath but a short time"* (Rev 12:12).

Concentration camp.

After the defeat of the devil and his angels in heaven, the earth became some sort of a concentration camp wherein they are now confined and from which they cannot escape. Question: Are not the fallen angels still spirits and beings of light? Escape from the earth should be quite easy.

The fallen angels may have lost many of their powers after being cast down to earth. They are beings of light, yes, but light, as physicists have found out, is affected by gravity. Gravitational force bends light, forcing it to travel in a curved path. The stronger the force of gravity, the more light is curved – until it can only travel in a circle – in short, trapped by gravity.

Albert Einstein's famous formula ($E = mc^2$) gave rise to the speculation that matter is simply trapped light energy. Quantum physicists have observed this in the process of electron-positron annihilation that produces photons: when energy is sufficiently high, these can turn back into matter and antimatter. That light energy can be transformed into matter is now an established scientific fact proven many times in the laboratory.[1]

To make a long story short, gravity has restricted the movements of the fallen angels, holding them captives on earth.

Beings beneath the earth.

In Philippians 2:10, we are instructed that everybody is to kneel on hearing the name of the Messiah – including those under the earth! *"That at the name of Jesus every knee should bow, of things in heaven, and things in earth, and things under the earth."* These obviously do no include dead people, who no longer move in the grave. (Incidentally, "Jesus" is not the real name of the Messiah, it is only the English transliteration of the Hebrew original we just saw on page 50.)

In Revelation 5:3, we also read that, *"And no man in heaven, nor in earth, neither under the earth, was able to open the book, neither to look thereon."* No human being, even one *"under the earth,"* will be able to open the book! John wrote as though he knew there were people living underground!

He continues with the same supposition in verse 5:13 -- *"And every creature which is in heaven, and on the earth, and under the earth, and such as are in the sea, and all that are in them, heard I saying, Blessing, and honour, and glory, and power, be unto him that sitteth upon the throne, and unto the Lamb for ever and ever."* He heard the voices of all creatures, including those *"under the earth,"* praising God and His Son.

Barnes Notes says: "[And things under the earth] Beings under the earth. The whole universe shall confess that he is Lord. This embraces, doubtless, those who have departed from this life, and perhaps includes also fallen angels."[2] It looks like many fallen angels have chosen to live underground. They then became the stuff of folklore and fairytales – pixies, elves, goblins, trolls, ogres, nymphs, and other fairy-like beings.

This must have stimulated the imagination of J.R.R. Tolkien (d. 1973), one of the translators of The Jerusalem Bible (1966), to write his widely popular fantasy trilogy, *The Lord of the Rings* (1954-55), about subterranean kingdoms in "Middle Earth."

How many angels in all?

If we are now the target of the wrath and malice of Satan and his demons, it will be helpful for us to know how many they are, as well as the heavenly angels who are on our side. A similar thought occurred to Job a little over 4,000 years ago. *"Is there any number of his armies?"* (Job 25:3a). Surprisingly, their numbers are in the Bible!

To start with, let us take account of the fact that the angels do not marry. So, they do not reproduce – their number is fixed. Let us look for more leads. We get a big help from Revelation 12:3-4b -- *"And there appeared another wonder in heaven; and behold a great red dragon, having seven heads and ten horns, and seven crowns upon his heads. And his tail drew the third part of the stars of heaven, and did cast them to the earth."*

The dragon, Satan, gathered a third of the stars (angels) to him If one-third of the angels are now with Satan… then two-thirds of the angels have remained with God.

Angelic guests.

We find the same ratio in a prophecy of "types" in Genesis: *"And the LORD appeared unto him in the plains of Mamre: and he sat in the tent door in the heat of the day; And he lift up his eyes and looked, and, lo, three men stood by him: and when he saw them, he ran to meet them from the tent door, and bowed himself toward the ground"* (Gen 18:1-2). Abraham prepared a repast of bread, veal, butter and milk for them. After eating, the three angels left for Sodom to see Lot, Abraham's nephew.

"And there came two angels to Sodom at even; and Lot sat in the gate of Sodom: and Lot seeing them rose up to meet them; and he bowed himself with his face toward the ground" (Gen 19:1). Did you notice? Lot greeted two angels, whereas three had earlier visited Abraham. One angel was gone.

The missing angel represents one-third of angels who joined Satan; the two stand for the two-thirds who have emained loyal to God. They are *"all the holy angels"* who will come with Christ at the time of the end (Matt 25:31). Lot is a "type" of the saved who will be taken up before the destruction of the earth. (*"But the same day that Lot went out of Sodom it rained fire and brimstone from heaven, and destroyed them all"* -- Luke 17:29).

Destroying angels from heaven.
In the parable of the tares, Christ prophesied that at the end of the world the angels will gather the wicked ones ("*tares*") first, ahead of the righteous ("*wheat*"). *"Let both grow together until the harvest: and in the time of harvest I will say to the reapers, Gather ye together first the tares, and bind them in bundles to burn them: but gather the wheat into my barn... As therefore the tares are gathered and burned in the fire; so shall it be in the end of this world. The Son of man shall send forth his angels, and they shall gather out of his kingdom all things that offend, and them which do iniquity; And shall cast them into a furnace of fire: there shall be wailing and gnashing of teeth."* (Matt 13:30,40-42).

"Day of the LORD." The angels will come on the "Day of the LORD." *"I have commanded my sanctified ones, I have also called my mighty ones for mine anger, even them that rejoice in my highness. The noise of a multitude in the mountains, like as of a great people; a tumultuous noise of the kingdoms of nations gathered together: the LORD of hosts mustereth the host of the battle. They come from a far country, from the end of heaven, even the LORD, and the weapons of his indignation, to destroy the whole land. Howl ye; for the day of the LORD is at hand; it shall come as a destruction from the Almighty... For the stars of heaven and the constellations thereof shall not give their light: the sun shall be darkened in his going forth, and the moon shall not cause her light to shine. And I will punish the world for their evil, and the wicked for their iniquity"* (Isa 13:3-6,10-11a). The Day of the LORD will be a day of darkness.

Destruction by fire. Isaiah's account is paralleled by Joel's. *"Blow ye the trumpet in Zion, and sound an alarm in my holy mountain: let all the inhabitants of the land tremble: for the day of the LORD cometh, for it is nigh at hand; A day of darkness and of gloominess, a day of clouds and of thick darkness, as the morning spread upon the mountains: a great people and a strong; there hath not been ever the like, neither shall be any more after it, even to the years of many generations. A fire devoureth before them; and behind them a flame burneth: the land is as the garden of Eden before them, and behind them a desolate wilderness; yea, and nothing shall escape them. The* *appearance of them is as the appearance of horses; and as horsemen, so shall they run"* (Joel 2:1-4).

Horse-like appearance. Strangely, the destroying angels from heaven will look like horses and horsemen. Then John tells us how many they are. *"And the number of the army of the horsemen were two hundred thousand thousand: and I heard the number of them. And thus I saw the horses in the vision, and them that sat on them, having breastplates of fire, and of jacinth, and brimstone: and the heads of the horses were as the heads of lions; and out of their mouths issued fire and smoke and brimstone. By these three was the third part of men killed..."* (Rev 9:16-18).

The first line completes the data we need. *"Two hundred thousand thousand"* (200 million). If the 200 million horsemen who will come on the Day of the LORD are the two-thirds of the angels who had remained with God, then the one-third who had joined Satan are... 100 million, right? Ergo, the total number of angels is 300 million!

The number of angels

Qty.	Description	Number
1/3	Angels with Satan	100 million
2/3	God's army from heaven	200 million
	Therefore…	
	Total number of angels	300 million

Some eschatologists think the 200 million horsemen are the "kings of the east" on their way to Armageddon, but the arrival of the angelic horsemen is signaled by the sixth trumpet (Rev 9:13-16), while the kings of the east allied with the Antichrist will not be coming until the sixth bowl or vial (Rev 16:12-16).

Several passages wherein actual incidents are also hidden prophecies appear to corroborate the 300 million number.

Gideon's 300.

In the book of Judges, Midianites raided Israel every harvest time for seven years, Finally, God told Gideon to muster volunteers to repulse the marauders. 32,000 Israelites answered the call to fight an army of 135,000 Midianites and their allies.

Trial by water. "*The LORD said to Gideon, "You have too many men for me to deliver Midian into their hands. In order that Israel may not boast against me that her own strength has saved her, announce now to the people, 'Anyone who trembles with fear may turn back and leave Mount Gilead.' So twenty-two thousand men left, while ten thousand remained. But the LORD said to Gideon, 'There are still too many men. Take them down to the water, and I will sift them for you there... 'Separate those who lap the water with their tongues like a dog from those who kneel down to drink.' Three hundred men lapped with their hands to their mouths. All the rest got down on their knees to drink. The LORD said to Gideon, 'With the three hundred men that lapped I will save you and give the Midianites into your hands....'"* (Judg 7:2-4b,5b-7, NIV)

The 300 who lapped the water from their palms were alert, watching out for enemies, while those who drank on their knees were oblivious to anything else. These were sent home. Later, using a clever ploy, Gideon and the 300 Israelites miraculously routed the 135,000-strong Midianite horde (Judg 7:16-22).

Add 6 zeroes. If we add 6 zeroes to each number, we get some interesting figures. Are the 32,000 all 32 billion humans who will have lived from creation to the Last Judgment? Are the 22,000 who would not fight 22 billion people who will never have engaged in wars? Are the 10,000 who stayed to fight 10 billion men who will have fought in wars from creation to Armageddon? And are the 300 God's 300 million angels?

A population explosion looks probable in the Millennium, as man's lifespan will return to pre-Flood levels (Isa 65:20-22) and long-living women will produce children for hundreds of years. Early in the 21st century, the media reported a scientific study showing that the Earth's resources can support a population of some 20 billion humans. (More in the Appendix.)

The kidnapping of Lot.

A scenario in Genesis seems to show that the 300 million number of angels is not a round figure. In verses 14:5-12, Amraphel, king of Shinar (a.k.a. Nimrod), took Lot captive. "*And when Abram heard that his brother was taken captive, he armed his trained servants, born in his own house, three* hundred and eighteen, and pursued them unto Dan. And he divided himself against them, he and his servants, by night, and smote them, and pursued them unto Hobah, which is on the left hand of Damascus."

The above incident is a prophecy of "types." Abram is a "type" or personification of God; "his trained servants," the angels; "his own house," heaven; that "he divided himself and his servants" was a prophecy that the angels would be divided. Thus, it looks like the more exact number of the angels is actually 318 million in all!

Eliezer, Abram's servant.

The head servant in Abram's household was Eliezer. *"And Abram said, Lord GOD, what wilt thou give me, seeing I go childless, and the steward of my house is this Eliezer of Damascus?"* (Gen 15:2). Eliezer means "help of God." (*El*, God; *ezer*, help) or "God's help." The angels are God's helpers.

Abram personifies God, while Eliezer is representative of the angels, God's helpers. Amazingly, the name "Eliezer" has a *gematria* (using letters as numbers) of 318, seemingly confirming that the original and total number of angels is 318 million!

Hebrew	Letter	English	Value
א	Aleph	E	1
ל	Lamed	L	30
י	Yod	I	10
ע	Ayin	E	70
ז	Zayin	Z	7
..		E*	
ר	Resh	R	200
			318

*Indicated by vowel points only

Fight or flight?

Now we know how many friends and foes we have. Fight or flight? Retreat or escape is futile, the enemy will follow and find us anywhere we go. So, let us learn all we can about them.

Enemy forces.

Let us assess the dark forces deployed against us. In 1 AD, just some 30 years before Satan and his angels were cast down to earth, the world population was estimated to have been around 300 million. So, when the demons fell to earth, the ratio of men to the fallen angels, whose number we have seen to be about 100 million, was around 3 to 1. Each demon had the job of causing three unwary people to sin by disobeying God. That was probably easy work for them. And though men multiplied – some 435 million in 1500, then 800 million in 1750 – the figures were still manageable for the demons, 4:1 then 8:1.

Even when the world population hit 1 billion in 1830, 10:1 was probably still child's play for them. But with the population exploding to 2 billion in 1930, 3 billion in 1961, 4 billion in 1978, 5 billion in 1987, 6 billion in 1999, and 7 billion in 2011, their malevolent work must have become increasingly difficult. Well, not really.

Mass deception.

We saw in Ezekiel 28:12 that Lucifer is supremely wise, and with his great intelligence he has made the work of his demons a lot easier. He established false religions and sinful churches all over the world, ensuring that generations after generations of men will be born to worship wrong gods in wrong ways.

The devil and his minions typically begin by sowing the seeds of erroneous notions and beliefs that, in time, become accepted as truths. *"Now the Spirit speaketh expressly, that in the latter times some shall depart from the faith, giving heed to seducing spirits, and doctrines of devils"* (1 Tim 4:1).

Their evil scheme is working. As we see today, children born to parents practicing spurious religious customs grow up doing the same things. Satan has little reason to worry that those deceived persons will later become spiritually saved.

Devil worship.

Isaiah 14:12-14 showed us that Lucifer wanted to be like God. It follows that he also wants people to worship him. Tempting Christ in the wilderness, he had the gall to ask the Son of God to prostrate Himself before him. *"And saith unto him, All these things will I give thee, if thou wilt fall down and worship me"* (Matt 4:9).

Misled people make offerings to demons. *"They sacrificed unto devils, not to God; to gods whom they knew not, to new gods that came newly up, whom your fathers feared not"* (Deut 32:17) – from OT to NT times -- *"What say I then? that the idol is any thing, or that which is offered in sacrifice to idols is any thing? But I say, that the things which the Gentiles sacrifice, they sacrifice to devils, and not to God: and I would not that ye should have fellowship with devils"* (1 Cor 10:20). Some even offered their children to demons. *"Yea, they sacrificed their sons and their daughters unto devils"* (Ps 106:37).

The devil and his demons have tricked countless people throughout the millennia into worshipping them. Apparently, the fallen angels inhabit graven images, so that when people kneel down and pray to those objects, they are paying homage to demons! *"And the rest of the men which were not killed by these plagues yet repented not of the works of their hands, that they should not worship devils, and idols of gold, and silver, and brass, and stone, and of wood: which neither can see, nor hear, nor walk"* (Rev 9:20).

Draconic divinity.

Satan, in one of his guises, is worshipped unknowingly by many people on earth. *"And they worshipped the dragon which gave power unto the beast"* (Rev 13:4).

All over the world, some ancient peoples had religions of one form or another that included the worship of serpents or dragons. The snake is a divinity in India. The dragon is venerated to this day in East Asia. In Central and South America, some people still await the return of Quetzalcoatl, the feathered serpent-god, who some believe was an extraterrestrial.

Covert operations

Except in a few rare instances, the devil and his demons do their work in secret. As much as possible, they do not want men to know they exist. The more people ignore or doubt their existence, the more successful their work becomes! In the Old Testament, before the Son of God came in the flesh to start the work of salvation, there were very few incidents involving demons or "unclean spirits." Their presence became well known only after Christ began His earthly ministry.

John says Satan was the reason why the Messiah came to earth. *"He that committeth sin is of the devil; for the devil sinneth from the beginning. For this purpose the Son of God was manifested, that he might destroy the works of the devil"* (1 John 3:8). Paul adds: *"How God anointed Jesus of Nazareth with the Holy Ghost and with power: who went about doing good, and healing all that were oppressed of the devil; for God was with him"* (Acts 10:38).

Modus operandi

Satan and his dark angels work in various ways to accomplish their objective. Here are some of the methods they use to lead us astray.

Putting ideas in people's minds.

The evil spirits often inject thoughts into our minds that we think are our own, but later regret. Let us look at some instances.

Peter. A little noticed incident was when Christ told the disciples about His impending death and Peter refused to accept it. *"Then Peter took him, and began to rebuke him, saying, Be it far from thee, Lord: this shall not be unto thee. But he turned, and said unto Peter, Get thee behind me, Satan: thou art an offence unto me: for thou savourest not the things that be of God, but those that be of men"* (Matt 16:22-23; cf. Mark 8:32-33). Christ knew Satan was putting the words in Peter's mouth and commanded the devil to go away.

Ananias. Rather than give Peter all the money from the sale of his property that had become communal, Ananias kept a part for himself. *"But Peter said, Ananias, why hath Satan filled thine heart to lie to the Holy Ghost, and to keep back part of the price of the land?"* (Acts 5:3). Peter knew Satan made Ananias do it.

Job. To test Job, God allowed Satan to do anything, except kill him. *"And the LORD said unto Satan, Behold, he is in thine hand; but save his life"* (Job 2:6). Guess who gave raiders the idea to steal his livestock and kill his servants. *"And there came a messenger unto Job, and said, The oxen were plowing, and the* *asses feeding beside them: And the Sabeans fell upon them, and took them away; yea, they have slain the servants with the edge of the sword; and I only am escaped alone to tell thee... While he was yet speaking, there came also another, and said, The Chaldeans made out three bands, and fell upon the camels, and have carried them away, yea, and slain the servants with the edge of the sword..."* (Job 1:14-15,17).

Armageddon. Evil spirits from Satan will induce the world leaders allied with the Antichrist to invade Israel for the last and greatest battle on earth. *"And I saw three unclean spirits like frogs come out of the mouth of the dragon, and out of the mouth of the beast, and out of the mouth of the false prophet. For they are the spirits of devils, working miracles, which go forth unto the kings of the earth and of the whole world, to gather them to the battle of that great day of God Almighty... And he gathered them together into a place called in the Hebrew tongue Armageddon"* (Rev 16:13-14,16).

A word of caution, though. Christ said many evil thoughts frequently come from our own minds, too. *"For out of the heart proceed evil thoughts, murders, adulteries, fornications, thefts, false witness, blasphemies"* (Matt 15:19).

Entering bodies.

Many times, not content with just putting ideas into people's minds, evil spirits enter and possess physical bodies!

People. Satan himself entered the body of Judas to ensure the execution of his plot. *"Jesus answered, He it is, to whom I shall give a sop, when I have dipped it. And when he had dipped the sop, he gave it to Judas Iscariot, the son of Simon. And after the sop Satan entered into him..."* (John 13:26-27a).

Some demons dabble in fortune-telling. *"And it came to pass, as we went to prayer, a certain damsel possessed with a spirit of divination met us, which brought her masters much gain by soothsaying"* (Acts 16:16). This is an abomination to God.

Possessed persons often act violently. *"And when he was come to the other side into the country of the Gergesenes, there met him two possessed with devils, coming out of the tombs, exceeding fierce, so that no man might pass by that way. And, behold, they cried out, saying, What have we to do with thee,*

Jesus, thou Son of God? art thou come hither to torment us before the time?" (Matt 8:28-29).

Surprisingly, more than one demon may possess a person. *"For he said unto him, Come out of the man, thou unclean spirit. And he asked him, What is thy name? And he answered, saying, My name is Legion: for we are many. And he besought him much that he would not send them away out of the country"* (Mark 5:8-10). A Roman legion had 3,000-6,000 men.

Animals. Animals are fair game to evil spirits. (Witches call these animals "familiars.") *"Now there was there nigh unto the mountains a great herd of swine feeding. And all the devils besought him, saying, Send us into the swine, that we may enter into them. And forthwith Jesus gave them leave. And the unclean spirits went out, and entered into the swine: and the herd ran violently down a steep place into the sea, (they were about two thousand;) and were choked in the sea"* (Mark 5:11-13). Some two thousand demons had possessed the man!

Causing infirmities and disabilities.

Modern doctors will probably laugh at this, but many illnesses were (and apparently still are) caused by evil spirits.

Deafness. *"When Jesus saw that the people came running together, he rebuked the foul spirit, saying unto him, Thou dumb and deaf spirit, I charge thee, come out of him, and enter no more into him. And the spirit cried, and rent him sore, and came out of him..."* (Mark 9:25-26a).

Muteness. *"As they went out, behold, they brought to him a dumb man possessed with a devil. And when the devil was cast out, the dumb spake: and the multitudes marvelled, saying, It was never so seen in Israel"* (Matt 9:32-33).

Blindness. *"Then was brought unto him one possessed with a devil, blind, and dumb: and he healed him, insomuch that the blind and dumb both spake and saw"* (Matt 12:22).

Deformities. *"And, behold, there was a woman which had a spirit of infirmity eighteen years, and was bowed together, and could in no wise lift up herself. And when Jesus saw her, he called her to him, and said unto her, Woman, thou art loosed from thine infirmity. And he laid his hands on her: and immediately she was made straight..."* (Luke 13:11-13).

Various diseases. *"And in that same hour he cured many of their infirmities and plagues, and of evil spirits; and unto many that were blind he gave sight"* (Luke 7:21).

Paul himself was afflicted. *"And lest I should be exalted above measure through the abundance of the revelations, there was given to me a thorn in the flesh, the messenger of Satan to buffet me, lest I should be exalted above measure"* (2 Cor 12:7). God, however, asked Paul to bear it in order to glorify Him. *"For this thing I besought the Lord thrice, that it might depart from me. And he said unto me, My grace is sufficient for thee: for my strength is made perfect in weakness"* (2 Cor 12:8-9a).

House-hunting demons.

Why do evil spirits possess people? *"When the unclean spirit is gone out of a man, he walketh through dry places, seeking rest, and findeth none. Then he saith, I will return into my house from whence I came out; and when he is come, he findeth it empty, swept, and garnished. Then goeth he, and taketh with himself seven other spirits more wicked than himself, and they enter in and dwell there: and the last state of that man is worse than the first.* (Matt 12:43-45; cf. Luke 11:24-26).

It appears demons can only shuttle back and forth between physical bodies and a parched wilderness (Gehenna?). No wonder they begged Christ *"that he would not send them away out of the country"* (Mark 5:10b).

Ages-old gambit

Satan has a gambit that he just keeps on repeating through the ages. John summarizes it for us: *"For all that is in the world, the lust of the flesh, and the lust of the eyes, and the pride of life, is not of the Father, but is of the world"* (1 John 2:16). The ploy consists of three parts: 1) lust of the flesh, 2) lust of the eyes, and 3) pride of life. Let us see how Satan uses these tricks.

Adam and Eve.

Satan used the stratagem from the very beginning – in Eden. *"And when the woman saw that the tree was good for food* (lust of the flesh)*, and that it was pleasant to the eyes* (lust of the eyes)*, and a tree to be desired to make one wise* (pride of life)*,* *she took of the fruit thereof, and did eat, and gave also unto her husband with her; and he did eat"* (Gen 3:6). It succeeded, resulting in the fall of Adam and, in effect, all of mankind.

Renegade angels.

Satan used it on the angels, too. *"And it came to pass, when men began to multiply on the face of the earth, and daughters were born unto them, That the sons of God saw the daughters of men that they were fair* (lust of the eyes); *and they took them wives of all which they chose* (lust of the flesh)... *There were giants in the earth in those days; and also after that, when the sons of God came in unto the daughters of men, and they bare children to them, the same became mighty men which were of old, men of renown* (pride of life).

Christ in the wilderness..

Satan's most prized target was the Son of God. *"And when he had fasted forty days and forty nights, he was afterward an hungred. And when the tempter came to him, he said, If thou be the Son of God, command that these stones be made bread* (lust of the flesh). *But he answered and said, It is written, Man shall not live by bread alone, but by every word that proceedeth out of the mouth of God. Then the devil taketh him up into the holy city, and setteth him on a pinnacle of the temple, And saith unto him, If thou be the Son of God, cast thyself down: for it is written, He shall give his angels charge concerning thee: and in their hands they shall bear thee up, lest at any time thou dash thy foot against a stone* (pride of life). *Jesus said unto him, It is written again, Thou shalt not tempt the Lord thy God. Again, the devil taketh him up into an exceeding high mountain, and sheweth him all the kingdoms of the world, and the glory of them* (lust of the eyes); *And saith unto him, All these things will I give thee, if thou wilt fall down and worship me"* (Matt 4:2-9; cf. Luke 4:2-11). Satan failed miserably this time.

Our end-time generation.

Men today must look like easy prey to Satan. *"But mark this: There will be terrible times in the last days. People will be lovers of themselves, lovers of money, boastful, proud, abusive, disobedient to their parents, ungrateful, unholy, without love, unforgiving, slanderous, without self-control, brutal, not lovers of the good, treacherous, rash, conceited, lovers of pleasure rather than lovers of God- having a form of godliness but denying its power"* (2 Tim 3:1-5a, NIV).

Let us break down the passage under each of the three baits Satan uses to see how he is beguiling the unwary in our midst: 1) Lust of the flesh – without self-control, lovers of pleasure rather than lovers of God; 2) Lust of the eyes – lovers of money, and 3) Pride of life -- lovers of themselves, boastful, proud, abusive, disobedient to their parents, ungrateful, unholy, without love, unforgiving, slanderous, brutal, not lovers of the good, treacherous, rash, conceited, having a form of godliness but denying its power. Notice these things happening today?

Match-ups

As we now know, angels have a hierarchy that ranks them according to power. Fallen angels still do, too. Paul says, *"For we wrestle not against flesh and blood, but against principalities, against powers, against the rulers of the darkness of this world, against spiritual wickedness in high places"* (Eph 6:12).

Since Paul was a leading apostle, we gather from the verse that the godlier a person is, the more powerful the demon that is matched against him or her! Remember Gabriel was unable to overcome the prince of Persia? Michael the archangel had to come and help him. *"But the prince of the kingdom of Persia withstood me one and twenty days: but, lo, Michael, one of the chief princes, came to help me..."* (Dan 10:13a).

Defense against the devil

Defending ourselves against the evil ones can be surprisingly simple. *"Submit yourselves therefore to God. Resist the devil, and he will flee from you"* (James 4:7).

Note, however, that it is not simply a matter of resisting the devil, we must also "submit ourselves to God." In other words, in order to fend off the forces of darkness, we must first be obedient to the will of our Father in heaven.

A way out. God also makes sure that all temptations thrown in our way by the devil will be within our ability to handle or overcome. *"There hath no temptation taken you but such as is common to man: but God is faithful, who will not suffer you to be tempted above that ye are able; but will with the temptation also make a way to escape, that ye may be able to bear it"* (1 Cor 10:13). After all, *"God hath not given us the spirit of fear; but of power, and of love, and of a sound mind"* (2 Tim 1:7).

Armor and weapon of God.

In addition to dodging and defying the devil, we have both armor and weapon from God. Paul instructs us: *"Put on the full armor of God so that you can take your stand against the devil's schemes... Stand firm then, with the belt of truth buckled around your waist, with the breastplate of righteousness in place, and with your feet fitted with the readiness that comes from the gospel of peace. In addition to all this, take up the shield of faith, with which you can extinguish all the flaming arrows of the evil one. Take the helmet of salvation and the sword of the Spirit, which is the word of God"* (Eph 6:11,14-17, NIV).

Do not take these instructions lightly as just figures of speech. We see Christ armed similarly. *"And out of his mouth goeth a sharp sword, that with it he should smite the nations: and he shall rule them with a rod of iron..."* (Rev 19:15a). That sword, as Paul says, is *"the sword of the Spirit, which is the word of God."* If we will recall, each time Satan tempted Christ in the wilderness, He responded with a passage from Scriptures, the word of God, defeating the devil.

Spiritual strike-back!

No one is spared from the attacks, the forces of darkness bedevil everybody. Fighting back is the best option we have. Let us see how Christ and His disciples battled the wicked ones.

Christ cast out demons

As the Son of God, with the Godhead indwelling Him (Col 2:9), Christ simply commanded the evil spirits. *"And there was in their synagogue a man with an unclean spirit; and he cried out, Saying, Let us alone; what have we to do with thee, thou Jesus of Nazareth? art thou come to destroy us? I know thee who thou art, the Holy One of God. And Jesus rebuked him, saying, Hold thy peace, and come out of him. And when the unclean spirit had torn him, and cried with a loud voice, he came out of him"* (Mark 1:23-26; cf. Luke 4:33-35; see also Matt 8:28-32; 12:22; Mark 9:17-27; Luke 7:21).

Disciples defeated demons.

Christ taught the disciples how to expel evil spirits from possessed persons. *"And when he had called unto him his twelve disciples, he gave them power against unclean spirits, to cast them out, and to heal all manner of sickness and all manner of disease.* (Matt 10:1; cf. Mark 6:7).

How? By using the power of the personal name of Christ. *"And these signs shall follow them that believe; In my name shall they cast out devils"* (Mark 16:17a). Paul did so, too. *"And this did she many days. But Paul, being grieved, turned and said to the spirit, I command thee in the name of Jesus Christ to come out of her. And he came out the same hour"* (Acts 16:18). The disciples were also very successful. *"And the seventy returned again with joy, saying, Lord, even the devils are subject unto us through thy name"* (Luke 10:17).

Interestingly, in an unexpected development, Paul became so imbued with the power of the Son of God that people were healed even without his presence! *"So that from his body were brought unto the sick handkerchiefs or aprons, and the diseases departed from them, and the evil spirits went out of them"* (Acts 19:12). Personal articles that came into contact with Paul became healing instruments!

Christ's real name.

Did the disciples use the name "Jesus" against evil spirits? We must remember that, although the New Testament books had been written in Greek, many of the disciples were Jews with Hebrew names. So was Christ.

Actually, "Jesus" is just a 17th century English/German/Spanish form transliterated from the medieval Latin "Iesus," from the Greek "Iesous," nominative case of "Iesou," from the Hebrew variant "Yeshu," from the popular 1st century Hebrew form "Yeshua," from the Exodus period form "Yehoshua" ("Jehoshua"), from the ancient Hebrew original "Yahushua"

("Yahu"/God, "*shua*"/saves). This will be documented at length in a succeeding volume of this series.

Tough cases

Not all people, not even some disciples, were able to use the power of the Messiah's name effectively. The father of a possessed child told Christ: *"Lord, have mercy on my son: for he is lunatick, and sore vexed: for ofttimes he falleth into the fire, and oft into the water. And I brought him to thy disciples, and they could not cure him"* (Matt 17:15-16).

Prayer and fasting. *"Then Jesus answered and said, O faithless and perverse generation, how long shall I be with you? how long shall I suffer you? bring him hither to me. And Jesus rebuked the devil; and he departed out of him: and the child was cured from that very hour. Then came the disciples to Jesus apart, and said, Why could not we cast him out? And Jesus said unto them, Because of your unbelief: for verily I say unto you, If ye have faith as a grain of mustard seed, ye shall say unto this mountain, Remove hence to yonder place; and it shall remove; and nothing shall be impossible unto you. Howbeit this kind goeth not out but by prayer and fasting.* (Matt 17:17-21; cf. Mark 9:14-29; Luke 9:38).

Worse results. Non-believers had worse results. *"Then certain of the vagabond Jews, exorcists, took upon them to call over them which had evil spirits the name of the Lord Jesus, saying, We adjure you by Jesus whom Paul preacheth. And there were seven sons of one Sceva, a Jew, and chief of the priests, which did so. And the evil spirit answered and said, Jesus I know, and Paul I know; but who are ye? And the man in whom the evil spirit was leaped on them, and overcame them, and prevailed against them, so that they fled out of that house naked and wounded"* (Acts 19:13-16).

Armageddon!

The spiritual war will reach a physical climax in the last and greatest battle on earth – Armageddon. *"And I saw the beast, and the kings of the earth, and their armies, gathered together to make war against him that sat on the horse, and against his army"* (Rev 19:19). The horseman is Christ,

Christ will make short work of the beast (Antichrist) and his allies. *"And the beast was taken, and with him the false prophet that wrought miracles before him, with which he deceived them that had received the mark of the beast, and them that worshipped his image. These both were cast alive into a lake of fire burning with brimstone. And the remnant were slain with the sword of him that sat upon the horse, which sword proceeded out of his mouth: and all the fowls were filled with their flesh"* (Rev 19:20-21).

Bottomless pit.
Following his defeat, Satan will be imprisoned for 1,000 years. *"And I saw an angel come down from heaven, having the key of the bottomless pit and a great chain in his hand. And he laid hold on the dragon, that old serpent, which is the Devil, and Satan, and bound him a thousand years, And cast him into the bottomless pit, and shut him up, and set a seal upon him, that he should deceive the nations no more, till the thousand years should be fulfilled: and after that he must be loosed a little season"* (Rev 20:1-3).

Satan's demons will follow their master. *"And it shall come to pass in that day, that the LORD shall punish the host of the high ones that are on high, and the kings of the earth upon the earth. And they shall be gathered together, as prisoners are gathered in the pit, and shall be shut up in the prison, and after many days shall they be visited"* (Isa 24:21-22). In this thinly veiled prophecy, *"that day"* refers to the day of the LORD at the Second Coming, which will coincide with Armageddon; *"the high ones on high"* are the fallen angels; their visitation *"after many days"* refers to the Last Judgment after the Millennium, the 1,000-year era of peace on earth.

The last uprising.
After the Millennium, Satan will be released from the pit and again foment trouble… for the very last time. *"And when the thousand years are expired, Satan shall be loosed out of his prison, And shall go out to deceive the nations which are in the four quarters of the earth, Gog and Magog, to gather them together to battle: the number of whom is as the sand of the sea.*

And they went up on the breadth of the earth, and compassed the camp of the saints about, and the beloved city: and fire came down from God out of heaven, and devoured them" (Rev 20:7-9). The last uprising will be short-lived.

Finally, Satan will be thrown into the real hell. *"And the devil that deceived them was cast into the lake of fire and brimstone, where the beast and the false prophet are, and shall be tormented day and night for ever and ever"* (Rev 20:10).

Intriguing questions

Several intriguing questions remain unanswered.

Why was Lucifer not punished soon after he aspired to be like God? Why was he allowed to continue with his evil ways?

After the resurrection, why did not the Messiah establish the kingdom of God on earth right away? Why must He stay in heaven until the restoration of all things (Acts 3:20-21)?

After the war in heaven, why were the devil and his angels cast down to earth, not into the lake of fire?

After the Second Coming, why will the devil and his demons be imprisoned temporarily in the bottomless pit for 1,000 years, instead of being thrown directly once and for all into the lake of fire? Why must the beast and false prophet precede them?

After the thousand-year Millennium, why will Satan be set loose again to lead another uprising against God?

Why do Satan and the fallen angels keep on preventing people from being spiritually saved? Do they hope to win against God? They probably realize they cannot. But why do they persist in what they are doing?

And, lastly, what is God waiting for?

5

The Heirs of Heaven

Come, ye blessed of my Father, inherit the kingdom prepared for you from the foundation of the world.

-- Matthew 25:34b

Men who will emerge victorious in the spiritual war on earth will inherit the kingdom of heaven. They are the faithful believers who will overcome our invisible evil adversaries.

Christ said the poor are specially favored to become heirs. *"And he lifted up his eyes on his disciples, and said, Blessed be ye poor: for yours is the kingdom of God"* (Luke 6:20).

God Himself has personally picked His future heirs. *"Listen, my beloved brethren: Has God not chosen the poor of this world to be rich in faith and heirs of the kingdom which He promised to those who love Him?"* (James 2:5-6, NKJV). God makes His chosen ones poor and needy so that they will seek Him and have the opportunity to be rich in faith.

Co-heirs with Christ

Yet, not only the poor, but all who give themselves wholly to Christ can become heirs. *"And if ye be Christ's, then are ye Abraham's seed, and heirs according to the promise"* (Gal 3:29).

Faithful believers who choose to follow in the footsteps of Christ can become children and heirs of God. *"The Spirit itself beareth witness with our spirit, that we are the children of God: And if children, then heirs; heirs of God, and joint-heirs with Christ; if so be that we suffer with him, that we may be also glorified together"* (Rom 8:16-17).

From being mere servants, we can look forward to inheriting all the riches of the kingdom of heaven. *"Wherefore thou art no more a servant, but a son; and if a son, then an heir of God through Christ"* (Gal 4:7).

This has been made possible by the sacrifice of Christ on the cross. *"Blessed be the God and Father of our Lord Jesus Christ, which according to his abundant mercy hath begotten us again unto a lively hope by the resurrection of Jesus Christ from the dead, To an inheritance incorruptible, and undefiled, and that fadeth not away, reserved in heaven for you"* (1 Peter 1:3-4).

Sealed with the Spirit. The faithful are indwelt by the Holy Spirit, as an earnest of the inheritance promised to believers. *"And you also were included in Christ when you heard the word of truth, the gospel of your salvation. Having believed, you were marked in him with a seal, the promised Holy Spirit, who is a deposit guaranteeing our inheritance until the redemption of those who are God's possession-to the praise of his glory"* (Eph 1:13-14, NIV).

Heirs are called "saints"

All the heirs of God are called "saints." *"But the saints of the most High shall take the kingdom, and possess the kingdom for ever, even for ever and ever... Until the Ancient of days came, and judgment was given to the saints of the most High; and the time came that the saints possessed the kingdom"* (Dan 7:18, 22). Translated from Hebrew *qadosh* ("holy or morally clean") and Greek *hagios* ("pure and morally blameless"), "saint" means a faithful believer who consecrates or sets himself or herself apart from the world to the worship and service of God.

Easy to become a saint?

In Paul's epistles, it sounds quite easy to become a "saint." All we have to do is believe and have faith in Christ. *"Unto the church of God which is at Corinth, to them that are sanctified in Christ Jesus, called to be saints, with all that in every place call upon the name of Jesus Christ our Lord, both theirs and ours"* (1 Cor 1:2). People anywhere who call on the true name of Christ can become saints. Is it really as simple as that?

Luke, the Bible historian, recorded: *"And they said, Believe on the Lord Jesus Christ, and thou shalt be saved, and thy house"* (Acts 16:31). Faith in Christ saves spiritually.

Incomplete knowledge.

Yet, Paul, in about 55 AD, wrote in his first letter to the converts in Corinth that: *"For we know in part, and we prophesy in part. But when that which is perfect is come, then that which is in part shall be done away"* (1 Cor 13:9-10).

Did that make you sit up? Paul said that, at that time, the knowledge of the apostles was still incomplete!

Two requisites.

Some forty years later, around 95 AD, John (the only apostle to die of old age) wrote the book of Revelation, whose contents had been shown to him by an angel sent by Christ from heaven (Rev 1:1). He penned in Revelation 14:12: *"Here is the patience of the saints: here are they that keep the commandments of God, and the faith of Jesus."*

That may come as a surprise to many. John wrote that the saints do two things, not just one:
1) Keep the commandments of God; and
2) Keep faith or believe in Christ.

Classes of saints

Do you think that those who will be saved – the saints – will all be equal in heaven? Most people think so. Yet, the Scriptures say otherwise. Let us examine one usually glossed over passage in the Scriptures.

Christ said in Matthew 5:19 -- *"Whosoever therefore shall break one of these least commandments, and shall teach men so, he shall be called least in the kingdom of heaven: but whosoever shall do and teach them, the same shall be called great in the kingdom of heaven."*

Would you believe that? In effect, Christ said not everyone will be equal in the kingdom of heaven: some will be called "least," others will be called "great."

Optional commandments.
The verse also strongly implies that if there are "least" commandments, then there are also "great" commandments. The "least" commandments appear to be optional, because those who violate them will find themselves in the kingdom of heaven just the same!

Nonetheless, it goes without saying that those who will be called "least" in the kingdom obey the great commandments; else, they will not be admitted into the kingdom at all.

The "least." The Bible provides textual proof that a number of saints will indeed be called "least" in the kingdom of God. *"For I say unto you, Among those that are born of women there is not a greater prophet than John the Baptist: but he that is least in the kingdom of God is greater than he"* (Luke 7:28).

Paul taught that a number of commandments – such as circumcision and the dietary laws -- were not compulsory and necessary for salvation. And so he admits that he will be called "least" in the kingdom. *"Unto me, who am less than the least of all saints, is this grace given, that I should preach among the Gentiles the unsearchable riches of Christ"* (Eph 3:8).

The "great." Others will be known as "great," even "greatest" in the kingdom. *"At the same time came the disciples unto Jesus, saying, Who is the greatest in the kingdom of heaven? And Jesus called a little child unto him, and set him in the midst of them, And said, Verily I say unto you, Except ye be converted, and become as little children, ye shall not enter into the kingdom of heaven. Whosoever therefore shall humble himself as this little child, the same is greatest in the kingdom of heaven"* (Matt 18:1-4; cf. 20:26; Mark 10:43; Luke 9:48).

What makes a little child special? A trusting and submissive spirit, perhaps? Or, in a nutshell, faith and obedience.

Two resurrections

Bible prophecy foretells two resurrections, the raising back to life of dead people from the grave. That makes us wonder. Since there will be two groups of saints – the "great" and the "least" – will one group be in the first resurrection, and the other in the second? Who will be in which?

First resurrection.
The first resurrection, sometimes also called "Rapture," will take place at the Second Coming of Christ. *"And he shall send his angels with a great sound of a trumpet, and they shall gather together his elect from the four winds, from one end of heaven to the other"* (Matt 24:31). Note that a special group of saints called the "elect" will be taken.

"This is the first resurrection. Blessed and holy is he that hath part in the first resurrection: on such the second death hath no power, but they shall be priests of God and of Christ, and shall reign with him a thousand years" (Rev 20:5b-6). The "elect" saints in the first resurrection "shall reign" with Christ. That means they will be kings under Christ, who will be the King of kings and Prince of Peace (Isa 9:6) during the Millennium.

The elect are the "great"? "Elect" means "specially chosen or selected." Does it mean that the elect, who will be taken up in the first resurrection, are those who will be called "great" in the kingdom of heaven?

Supernatural bodies. The elect saints will acquire a new, supernatural kind of body. *"I declare to you, brothers, that flesh and blood cannot inherit the kingdom of God, nor does the perishable inherit the imperishable"* (1 Cor 15:50, NIV). It will be some sort of a non-physical body. *"It is sown a natural body; it is raised a spiritual body. There is a natural body, and there is a spiritual body"* (1 Cor 15:44).

The new bodies of the elect will be indestructible and deathless. *"Behold, I shew you a mystery; We shall not all sleep, but we shall all be changed, In a moment, in the twinkling of an eye, at the last trump: for the trumpet shall sound, and the dead shall be raised incorruptible, and we shall be changed. For this corruptible must put on incorruption, and this mortal must put on immortality"* (1 Cor 15:51-53).

John says those bodies will be like Christ's own body. *"Beloved, now are we the sons of God, and it doth not yet appear what we shall be: but we know that, when he shall appear, we shall be like him; for we shall see him as he is"* (1 John 3:2). Paul wholeheartedly agrees: *"But our citizenship is in heaven. And we eagerly await a Savior from there, the Lord Jesus Christ, who, by the power that enables him to bring everything under his control, will transform our lowly bodies so that they will be like his glorious body"* (Phil 3:20-21, NIV).

Job knew about that future transformation more than 4,000 years ago. *"If a man die, shall he live again? all the days of my appointed time will I wait, till my change come"* (Job 14:14).

Second resurrection

The second resurrection will occur after about 1,000 years – for the Last Judgment in front of the Great White Throne of God. *"But the rest of the dead lived not again until the thousand years were finished... And I saw the dead, small and great, stand before God; and the books were opened: and another book was opened, which is the book of life: and the dead were judged out of those things which were written in the books, according to their works"* (Rev 20:5a,12).

Only the damned? Some denominations teach that only sinners will be brought back to life in the second resurrection. According to their doctrine, all of the saved people will have been taken earlier in the first resurrection.

The New Unger's Bible Dictionary appears to support the doctrine: "Thus during the present church age, the redeemed who die are 'absent from the body... at home with the Lord.; The wicked, by contrast, are in hades. Both are awaiting resurrection: one the resurrection to life and the other the resurrection to condemnation."[1] It then sums up the doctrine: "The resurrection of the righteous will take place at the coming of Christ (1 Thess 4:13-18; 1 Cor 15:53), of the unsaved at the great white throne judgment after the Kingdom age (Rev 2:11-15)."[2] Yet, the proof-texts seem rather inadequate.

Both saved and damned. On the other hand, there are other passages that quite clearly point to a general resurrection of both the saved and the damned, such as Daniel 12:2 -- *"And many of them that sleep in the dust of the earth shall awake, some to everlasting life, and some to shame and everlasting contempt."* The same is true with Acts 24:15 -- *"And have hope* toward God, which they themselves also allow, that there shall be a resurrection of the dead, both of the just and unjust."

John 5:28-29 is more specific. *"Marvel not at this: for the hour is coming, in the which all that are in the graves shall hear his voice, And shall come forth; they that have done good, unto the resurrection of life; and they that have done evil, unto the resurrection of damnation."* Note that those who have done good and those who have done evil will come forth from the graves in the same hour!

Post-Millennial saints. Here is further evidence: We know that all those who will be saved as heirs of the kingdom of heaven are called "saints." Yet, many saints will still be on earth after the Millennium, long after the first resurrection! *"And when the thousand years are expired, Satan shall be loosed out of his prison, And shall go out to deceive the nations which are in the four quarters of the earth, Gog and Magog, to gather them together to battle: the number of whom is as the sand of the sea. And they went up on the breadth of the earth, and compassed the camp of the saints about"* (Rev 20:7-9a).

The rebels led by Satan will surround the "camp of the saints." Obviously, since the first resurrection will have already taken place 1,000 years earlier, these post-Millennial saints will be part of the second resurrection!

The rest are "least." A picture emerges. All the saints make up one big body of all those who will be saved. The elect who will be taken in the first resurrection are a special, elite group of saints within that body. The rest of the saints will be brought back to life 1,000 years later in the second resurrection.

Hence, these remaining saints, both dead and living, who will be in the second resurrection, are those who will be called "least" in the kingdom of heaven!

In the entire Bible, in both the Old and New Testaments, the word "elect" occurs only 17 times; while "saints" can be seen in a total of 96 instances. This suggests that the elect is a much smaller group within the great body of saints.

Jewish belief in resurrection

Jewish historian Flavius Josephus concurs with Christian doctrine: "This is the discourse concerning Hades, wherein the souls of all men are confined until a proper season, which God hath determined, when he will make a resurrection of all men from the dead, not procuring a transmigration of souls from one body to another, but raising again those very bodies..."[3]

He adds graphic details, such as Jews "believe that God is able, when he hath raised to life that body which was made a compound of the same elements, to make it immortal... We have therefore believed that the body will be raised again; for although it be dissolved, it is not perished; for the earth receives its remains, and preserves them... but at the mighty sound of God the Creator, it will sprout up, and be raised in a clothed and glorious condition... for although it be dissolved for a time on account of the original transgression, it exists still, and is cast into the earth as into a potter's furnace, in order to be formed again, not in order to rise again such as it was before, but in a state of purity, and so as never to be destroyed any more; and to everybody shall its own soul be restored; and when it has clothed itself with that body, it will not be subject to misery, but being itself pure, it will continue with its pure body, and rejoice with it..."[4] Josephus's account agrees with those of the Judeo-Christian Scriptures.

He continues, "...but as for the unjust, they will receive their bodies not changed, but with the same diseases wherein they died, and such as they were in their unbelief, the same shall they be when they shall be faithfully judged."[5]

The "elect" identified

Who are the "elect" -- God's chosen ones? We are told very plainly and directly in Isaiah 45:4, *"For Jacob my servant's sake, and Israel mine elect, I have even called thee by thy name: I have surnamed thee, though thou hast not known me."* God, speaking through the prophet, said Israel is His "elect."

About 750 years earlier, the LORD said the same thing, in so many words, to the Israelites through Moses. *"For thou art an holy people unto the LORD thy God: the LORD thy God hath chosen thee to be a special people unto himself, above all people that are upon the face of the earth"* (Deut 7:6).

God has selected Israel for a very special purpose. *"But you are a chosen people, a royal priesthood, a holy nation, a people belonging to God, that you may declare the praises of him who called you out of darkness into his wonderful light"* (1 Peter 2:9-10, NIV). Israelites are to be priests serving and praising God.

Israel replaced?

In our modern age, many theologians and church leaders claim that Israel has already been replaced as the elect of God! It is supposedly supported by a statistic, "A dominant majority (85%) of evangelical Christian churches today subscribe to the doctrine called 'Replacement Theology,' which teaches that the Church has replaced Israel in God's plan of salvation."[6]

The idea must have arisen from verses like Romans 2:28-29, wherein Paul says that *"he is not a Jew, which is one outwardly; neither is that circumcision, which is outward in the flesh: But he is a Jew, which is one inwardly; and circumcision is that of the heart, in the spirit, and not in the letter."* Accordingly, one who is Jewish by race and circumcised physically, is not considered a real Jew if he is not circumcised spiritually in his heart. On the other hand, a believer who is circumcised in the spirit, although he may be a Gentile by blood, is the true Jew.

Spiritual Israel. In short, the Israel that will be saved and become heirs of the kingdom of God is said to be no longer the nation of Jews genetically descended from Jacob, but rather the "Israel of God" – spiritual Israel. *"For in Christ Jesus neither circumcision availeth anything, nor uncircumcision, but a new creature. And as many as walk according to this rule, peace be on them, and mercy, and upon the Israel of God"* (Gal 6:15-16).

Another verse cited as evidence by Replacement theologians is Romans 11:17, which says that *"if some of the branches be broken off, and thou, being a wild olive tree, wert graffed in among them, and with them partakest of the root and fatness of the olive tree."* The unbelieving Jews, the natural branches of the olive tree (Israel), have been cut off and replaced with wild olive tree branches, the Gentile Christians.

However, they overlook the fact that the olive tree is still the same tree (that is, Israel)! In reality, it is the grafted branches from wild olive trees (the Gentile Christians) who have become parts and members of the original olive tree. Spiritually circumcised Gentiles are now Jews!

God does not change.

Did God change His mind? He unconditionally pledges in Psalm 89:34 -- *"My covenant will I not break, nor alter the thing that is gone out of my lips."* He further declares in Malachi 3:6a -- *"For I am the LORD, I change not..."*

Israel continues to be God's chosen people. *"God did not reject his people, whom he foreknew. Don't you know what the Scripture says in the passage about Elijah -- how he appealed to God against Israel: 'Lord, they have killed your prophets and torn down your altars; I am the only one left, and they are trying to kill me'? And what was God's answer to him? 'I have reserved for myself seven thousand who have not bowed the knee to Baal.' So too, at the present time there is a remnant chosen by grace"* (Rom 11:2-5, NIV). Their number may have decreased, but Israel, or more precisely Israel's remnant, is still God's elect.

Remnant of Israel.

In the Revelation, we get a description of what makes the remnant of Israel the elect of God. *"And the dragon was wroth with the woman, and went to make war with the remnant of her seed, which keep the commandments of God, and have the testimony of Jesus Christ"* (Rev 12:17).

Have we not read that somewhere before? Why, yes! Like the saints in Revelation 14:12, the "remnant of her seed" (Israel, God's elect) do the same two things:

1) Keep the commandments of God; and
2) Have the testimony (teachings) of Christ.

So, the two groups – the saints and the remnant of Israel – are the same? Yes, and no. Yes, because the remnant of Israel is also made up of saints, who are heirs that will be saved. No, because the remnant of Israel is the elect, the elite group within the great body of saints.

What sets them apart is, while the elect keep both the great and least commandments of God, the rest of the other saints obey only the great commandments, not the least commandments, which are optional (Matt 5:19). To put it succinctly, all of the elect are saints, but not all of the saints are elect.

The remnant of Israel who obey all the commandments of God and believe in Christ are known today as Messianic Jews.

Mysterious number

Many Christians have long known one mysterious number in Revelation. *"And I saw another angel ascending from the east, having the seal of the living God: and he cried with a loud voice to the four angels, to whom it was given to hurt the earth and the sea, Saying, Hurt not the earth, neither the sea, nor the trees, till we have sealed the servants of our God in their foreheads. And I heard the number of them which were sealed: and there were sealed an hundred and forty and four thousand of all the tribes of the children of Israel"* (Rev 7:2-4). No one knew what the number stood for, giving rise to various conjectures.

The 144,000.

Some say this is the total number of individuals who will be saved; others, the number of righteous churches; still others, the number of the faithful who will be divinely protected during the Great Tribulation; *Matthew Henry's Commentary,* "the remnant of that people which God had reserved according to the election of grace."[7] This last appears to be closest to the mark.

The mysterious group of 144,000 seems to be the remnant of Israel – the elect! The succeeding verses in Revelation 7:5-8 list down the twelve tribes of Israel. *"Of the tribe of Juda were sealed twelve thousand. Of the tribe of Reuben were sealed twelve thousand. Of the tribe of Gad were sealed twelve thousand. Of the tribe of Aser were sealed twelve thousand. Of the tribe of Nepthalim were sealed twelve thousand. Of the tribe of Manasses were sealed twelve thousand. Of the tribe of Simeon were sealed twelve thousand. Of the tribe of Levi were sealed twelve thousand. Of the tribe of Issachar were sealed twelve thousand. Of the tribe of Zabulon were sealed twelve thousand. Of the tribe of Joseph were sealed twelve thousand. Of the tribe of Benjamin were sealed twelve thousand."*

The prophecy in Romans 11:26a will thus be fulfilled. *"And so all Israel shall be saved: as it is written."* The whole nation of Israel will be saved -- not all Israelites individually, but all the twelve tribes of Israel.

Israelite bachelors only? Revelation 14:3-4 reads: *"And they sung as it were a new song before the throne, and before the four beasts, and the elders: and no man could learn that* song but the hundred and forty and four thousand, which were redeemed from the earth. These are they which were not defiled with women; for they are virgins. These are they which follow the Lamb whithersoever he goeth. These were redeemed from among men, being the firstfruits unto God and to the Lamb."*

Almost all who have read the verse wonder why only single Israelite men will be in the very special group of the one hundred forty-four thousand. The verse is not literal, though.

Prophetic symbols. We must remember that Revelation is a book of prophecy with many esoteric symbols that can be explained by the Bible itself. For instance, as we know already, a "woman" is the symbol of a faith or religion. So, the phrase "not defiled with women" means they are not tainted by the erroneous teachings of false churches. That they are "virgins" means they are spiritually pure and chaste. We become "virgins" by being born again through baptism in water (John 3:1-8). As Paul says, *"For I am jealous over you with godly jealousy: for I have espoused you to one husband, that I may present you as a chaste virgin to Christ"* (2 Cor 11:2). He was addressing all Christians; so "virgins" here refers to both men and women, Jews and Gentiles. Being the "firstfruits" redeemed from among men unto God and to the Lamb means they are the first ones – the elect -- who will be taken in the first resurrection.

Gentiles become elect, too

Gentile Christians can also become members of the elect. They are called such in Colossians 3:11-12 -- *"Where there is neither Greek nor Jew, circumcision nor uncircumcision, Barbarian, Scythian, bond nor free: but Christ is all, and in all. Put on therefore, as the elect of God, holy and beloved, bowels of mercies, kindness, humbleness of mind, meekness, long-suffering."* Paul says there is no deterrent – race, custom, social standing – for anyone to become a member of the elect.

Peter makes the same point, *"Peter, an apostle of Jesus Christ, to the strangers scattered throughout Pontus, Galatia, Cappadocia, Asia, and Bithynia, Elect according to the foreknowledge of God the Father, through sanctification of the Spirit"* (1 Peter 1:1-2a). He adds the thought that God already knows beforehand those who will be part of the elect.

THE HEIRS OF HEAVEN | 83

Naturalized Israelites.

In effect, Gentile Christians who are taken into the fold of the elect become "naturalized Israelites" spiritually. *"That at that time ye were without Christ, being aliens from the commonwealth of Israel, and strangers from the covenants of promise, having no hope, and without God in the world... Now therefore ye are no more strangers and foreigners, but fellowcitizens with the saints, and of the household of God"* (Eph 2:12,19).

Kings under Christ.

The 144,000 will be kings during the Millennium -- under Christ who will reign as the King of Kings.

Each and very one of them will receive a crown, as the Bible promises. 2 Timothy 4:8 -- *"Henceforth there is laid up for me a crown of righteousness, which the Lord, the righteous judge, shall give me at that day: and not to me only, but unto all them also that love his appearing";* James 1:12 -- *"Blessed is the man that endureth temptation: for when he is tried, he shall receive the crown of life, which the Lord hath promised to them that love him";* 1 Peter 5:4 -- *"And when the chief Shepherd shall appear, ye shall receive a crown of glory that fadeth not away";* Rev 2:10b -- *"...be thou faithful unto death, and I will give thee a crown of life."*

The jurisdictions of each of the 144,000 elect kings could be like the ones Christ illustrated in a parable. *"And he said unto him, Well, thou good servant: because thou hast been faithful in a very little, have thou authority over ten cities. And the second came, saying, Lord, thy pound hath gained five pounds. And he said likewise to him, Be thou also over five cities"* (Luke 19:17-19). How many cities do you think you will rule over, Your Royal Highness?

144,000 subjects each? There is speculation, based on the story of Gideon (Judges 7), that each of the 144,000 kings, on average, will rule over 144,000 subjects, too! Should that be the case, the total human population of the world during the Millennium would be around 21 billion.

As we have seen earlier, in the early years of the 21st century the media reported a scientific study showing that the Earth's resources can support a population of some 20 billion humans.

Number of the saints

We have seen how many the elect will be. Could we possibly find the total number of saints in the Bible, too? Since the Scriptures do not provide that information directly, we must again scrutinize the tell-tale verses step by step.

Predetermined number?

For starters, one verse seems to say that a predetermined number of saved men and women has to be completed. *"And when he had opened the fifth seal, I saw under the altar the souls of them that were slain for the word of God, and for the testimony which they held: And they cried with a loud voice, saying, How long, O Lord, holy and true, dost thou not judge and avenge our blood on them that dwell on the earth? And white robes were given unto every one of them; and it was said unto them, that they should rest yet for a little season, until their fellowservants also and their brethren, that should be killed as they were, should be fulfilled"* (Rev 6:9-11).

Petah Tikvah ("Door of Hope") magazine publisher-editor Rick 'Aharon' Chamberlin comments: "white robes are given to the martyrs under the altar. The martyrs are told to wait 'until their fellowservants also and their brethren who were to be killed even as they had been, should be complete also.' There is apparently a 'fullness of number' of martyrs which cannot be exceeded, as per Revelation 6:11. When the number is reached, then it sets in motion the events that transpire afterwards in the Scroll (Book) of Revelation."[8]

Paul reinforces that impression with a prophecy in Romans 11:25 – *"For I would not, brethren, that ye should be ignorant of this mystery, lest ye should be wise in your own conceits; that blindness in part is happened to Israel, until the fulness of the Gentiles be come in."* He says the Jews will not fully realize that they have rejected their long-awaited Messiah until the number of non-Jewish believers shall have been completed!

Saints before God's throne.

In Revelation 7:9,14b-15, John gives us a glimpse of a throng of people who will be saved – the saints. *"After this I beheld, and, lo, a great multitude, which no man could number, of all nations, and kindreds, and people, and tongues, stood before the throne, and before the Lamb, clothed with white robes, and palms in their hands... These are they which came out of great tribulation, and have washed their robes, and made them white in the blood of the Lamb. Therefore are they before the throne of God, and serve him day and night in his temple: and he that sitteth on the throne shall dwell among them."*

The saints are standing in front of the throne of God in heaven, holding and waving palms.

Old Testament number.

A little-noticed Biblical number comes to mind. We recall a likely figure in the book of Daniel. *"I beheld till the thrones were cast down, and the Ancient of days did sit, whose garment was white as snow, and the hair of his head like the pure wool: his throne was like the fiery flame, and his wheels as burning fire. A fiery stream issued and came forth from before him: thousand thousands ministered unto him, and ten thousand times ten thousand stood before him: the judgment was set, and the books were opened."* (Dan 7:9-10).

In this Old Testament book, among the millions (*"thousand thousands"*) serving God, we see a particular group of *"ten thousand times ten thousand"* (100,000,000 or one hundred million) also standing before God. Curiously, they are mentioned separately, as though very special.

New Testament number.

Surprisingly, we see that same number again in the very last book of the Bible. We read in Revelation 5:11 -- *"And I beheld, and I heard the voice of many angels round about the throne and the beasts and the elders: and the number of them was ten thousand times ten thousand, and thousands of thousands."* In this New Testament book, the very special group of *"ten thousand times ten thousand"* (100 million) is again mentioned separately, apart from the other *"thousands of thousands"* (millions) around the throne of God!

From these passages, one astounding conclusion crystallizes: the special group before the throne of God is made up of those who will be saved – the saints – 100 million in all!

The saints and the elect

We are blessed. We now have the complete picture: It looks like all the saints who will be saved will total one hundred million (100,000,000). Within that big group is a small, elite group of saints: the one hundred forty-four thousand (144,000) elect. With God's blessings, let us summarize and illustrate the distinctions between them in the table below:

Class	Commandments kept	Resurrection	Identity	Number
"Great"	Great and least	First	Elect (Israel)	144,000
"Least"	Great only	Second	Saints (Gentiles)	100 million

Identical number.

Come to think of it, have we not encountered the "100 million" number earlier in this book?

Strangely, yes. That figure is also the number of the fallen angels who joined Satan, remember? What an uncanny coincidence! But nothing ever happens by coincidence according to the Bible (Luke 12:6-7, etc.). So, God must have a special reason for the repetition of the number.

Saints equal to angels

Christ taught in Luke 20:35-36 -- *"But they which shall be accounted worthy to obtain that world, and the resurrection from the dead, neither marry, nor are given in marriage: Neither can they die any more: for they are equal unto the angels; and are the children of God, being the children of the resurrection."*

The thought is repeated in Matthew 22:30 -- *"For in the resurrection they neither marry, nor are given in marriage, but are as the angels of God in heaven"* (cf. Mark 12:25). The saints will be like angels!

The Book of Enoch (50:4) says the same thing: "In those days the mountains shall skip like rams, and the hills shall leap like young sheep (46) satiated with milk; and all the righteous shall become like angels in heaven."

The righteous become stars.
Another passage in the pseudepigraphal book relates. "I beheld another splendour, and the stars of heaven... Splendour produced splendour; and their conversion was into the number of the angels, and of the faithful. Then I inquired of the angel, who proceeded with me, and explained to me secret things, What their names were. He answered. A similitude of those has the Lord of spirits shown you. They are names of the righteous who dwell upon earth, and who believe in the name of the Lord of spirits for ever and for ever" (Book of Enoch 43:1,2).

That is astonishing. The number of the stars is equal to the number of the angels and the faithful! And the names of the stars are also the names of the righteous people on earth who call on the name of God – in short, the men and women who will be saved, the saints! Will they dwell in the stars just like the angels? Or, to call a spade a spade, will the saints become angels, too?

New sons of God

We learned in the beginning of this book that the angels are the "sons of God" (Job 38:7). Yet, in Romans 8:19 (NIV), Paul talks about the appearance of new "sons of God.": *"The creation waits in eager expectation for the sons of God to be revealed."* The angels have already been revealed to us. What other *"sons of God"* is Paul talking about?

He himself answers it for us in Romans 8:14: *"For as many as are led by the Spirit of God, they are the sons of God."* So, Spirit-led believers will also become sons of God! God promises it: *"And will be a Father unto you, and ye shall be my sons and daughters, saith the Lord Almighty"* (2 Cor 6:18). The saints will become children of God together with the angels!

The adversities that we experience in life are mere signs that we are being prepared to become sons of God. *"If ye endure chastening, God dealeth with you as with sons; for what son is he whom the father chasteneth not?"* (Heb 12:7).

Adopted sons.
Through Christ, God will adopt the saints as His sons -- *"he predestined us to be adopted as his sons through Jesus Christ, in accordance with his pleasure and will"* (Eph 1:5-6, NIV).

The Israelites will be adopted first and foremost -- *"the people of Israel. Theirs is the adoption as sons; theirs the divine glory, the covenants, the receiving of the law, the temple worship and the promises"* (Rom 9:4-5, NIV).

The saints will have the blessed privilege of calling on the Father most intimately. *"For ye have not received the spirit of bondage again to fear; but ye have received the Spirit of adoption, whereby we cry, Abba, Father"* (Rom 8:15).

The devil and demons disowned

After their defeat in their last uprising against God after the close of the Millennium (Rev 20:7-9), Satan and the fallen angels will at last be *"cast into the lake of fire and brimstone, where the beast and the false prophet are"* (Rev 20:10) -- the fate that they so justly deserve and has so long awaited them. (See also Matt 8:29 and 25:41.) The devil will be in good (or shall we say, bad?) company.

Let us now address a nagging question. Why did God wait until after the end of the Millennium to disown and destroy the devil and his demonic minions?

Fixed number of angels

As we have seen before, angels *"neither marry, nor are given in marriage"* (Matt 22:30; Mark 12:25) and so do not reproduce or multiply. Being immortal spirit and light, neither do they die (Luke 20:36). Therefore, their number is fixed – angels neither increase nor decrease.

God created them by the sound of His voice. *"By the word of the LORD were the heavens made; and all the host of them by the breath of his mouth"* (Ps 33:6). He *"commanded, and they were created. He hath also stablished them for ever and ever: he hath made a decree which shall not pass"* (Ps 148:5-6).

God does not change, *"For I am the LORD, I change not..."* (Mal 3:6), so He will not take back anything He has said. *"My covenant will I not break, nor alter the thing that is gone out of my lips"* (Ps 89:34).

Does it mean that if God had said at the creation that there would be 318 million angels, then the number of the angels will always be 318 million?

Fullness of the saints

After the Millennium, saints will still be in their camp that Satan's rebels will surround in the last uprising. That means the number of the saints in heaven will not have been completed yet by that time. When the devil and his demons are finally thrown into the lake of fire, we can conclude that no less than 100 million saints shall have already taken their place.

Now we know why Satan and his fiendish friends do not want people to be saved: Once the full number of the 100 million saints is completed, they are the ones who will be thrown into the lake of fire and brimstone! Good riddance.

Intuitive individuals

The notion that the saints will replace the fallen angels has occurred to quite a few Christian writers and visionaries. Let us get acquainted with these handful of intuitive individuals.

Emil Gaverluk.

Chrisitan author Dr. Emil Gaverluk "suggested that the number of angels who rebelled to follow Satan and leave their created order would be the same number in the Church at the Rapture. We read about the fullness of the Gentiles in Scripture and the translation of the Church. It was Dr. Gaverluk's theory that when the number of the Church (those saved during this dispensation of grace) reached the number of the angels who rebelled and fell, then that would determine the time of the Rapture"[9] Unfortunately, however, he did not find any scriptural support for his conjecture.

Saint Augustine.

One of the great leaders of the early Christian church, Saint Augustine (354-430) advanced the opinion that "the redeemed were elected by God to fill up the lapsed places in the heavenly hierarchy, occasioned by the fall of Satan and his demons."[10]

He wrote in his 5th century work *The City of God*: "It is He who made also man himself upright, with the same freedom of will—an earthly animal, indeed, but fit for heaven if he remained faithful to his Creator, but destined to the misery appropriate to such a nature if he forsook Him. It is He who, when He foreknew that man would in his turn sin by abandoning God and breaking His law, did not deprive him of the power of free-will, because He at the same time foresaw what good He Himself would bring out of the evil, and how from this mortal race, deservedly and justly condemned, He would by His grace collect, as now He does, a people so numerous, that He thus fills up and repairs the blank made by the fallen angels, and that thus that beloved and heavenly city is not defrauded of the full number of its citizens, but perhaps may even rejoice in a still more overflowing population...."[11]

Ellen G. White.

The Seventh-Day Adventist leader and prophetess Ellen G. White (1827-1915), was amply quoted by Pastor Jan Marcussen in his bi-monthly newsletter. "Then I saw a very great number of angels bring from the city glorious crowns – a crown for every saint, with his name written thereon.' ...Though the number is small compared to the many billions of the wicked of all ages, it is still 'a very great number.' You've already learned that the number of saints will be the same as the number of vacancies left by the fallen angels so that we will 'repopulate heaven.' Here's the quote, "It was God's purpose to repopulate heaven with the human family.' *God's Amazing Grace*, p. 344. We will fill up the vacancies left by the fallen angels.

"'*They shall be Mine, saith the LORD of hosts, in that day when I make up my jewels.*' Mal 3:17. Notice the words, 'make up.' Soon, the number of jewels will be made up. As soon as that 'very great number' is made up, Jesus will come and take us home to fill those vacancies. Is it really true that the vacancies made by the fall of Satan and his host will be filled by the redeemed of the Lord? Here's the quote – 'Heaven will triumph, for the vacancies made by the fall of Satan and his host will be filled by the redeemed of the Lord.' *Upward Look*, p. 61. That's why – by getting God's message to the people, we have it in our power to 'hasten' the Coming of Christ! (II Peter 3:12)... And that's why Jesus could have come in Sister White's day (6T 450) to 'repopulate heaven' if they had done their work so that the number of the jewels would have been made up in their day. That work has now fallen to us because in their day, there were not yet enough saints to fill those vacancies in heaven. If they had done it, the number of God's 'jewels' would have been 'made up,' and you and I would have never been born."[12]

Cindy Jacobs.

Founder of prayer network Generals of Intercession and called "prophet to the nations," Cindy Jacobs was one of the speakers on October 27, 2001, at "Catch the Fire" conference of Harvest International Ministries in California. In a high, clear, commanding voice, the words were said to have gushed out of her in a torrent without pause.

Prophesying on the Philippines, she spoke about the end of corruption in government, the guerrilla insurgency, awakening among the young military, the discovery of oil under the sea, "And the Lord says, 'Do not think I do not see you, Philippines, for I see you. You are the apple of my eye. You are a treasure unto me... Look to the University in Manila,' says God. 'For I will bring a revival that the... 'oh my Lord... the Lord says, 'The hundred thousand and thousand are going to get saved!'" She then picked up where she left off. "The Lord says, 'Can I touch a whole university? Yes. I can touch a whole university. I can come with my glory and I can come with my power in ways that you cannot imagine, for I am coming,' says God, 'I am coming and I will remain,' says the Lord.'"[13]

The number Cindy Jacobs exclaimed, "hundred thousand and thousand," can be written as "100,000,000" (one hundred million). Did she have a fleeting prophetic glimpse of the "*ten thousand times ten thousand*" standing before the throne of God? We can only wait in breathless expectation.

Few will be saved?

Some people wonder -- or are even skeptical – why only one hundred million persons will be saved, out of the many billions of humans who will have ever lived and died.

We cannot blame them. Some of the first century disciples felt that way, too. *"Then said one unto him, Lord, are there few that be saved?"* Christ did not answer him directly. *"And he said unto them, Strive to enter in at the strait gate: for many, I say unto you, will seek to enter in, and shall not be able"* (Luke

13:23-24). The answer is completed in another gospel: *"Enter ye in at the strait gate: for wide is the gate, and broad is the way, that leadeth to destruction, and many there be which go in thereat: Because strait is the gate, and narrow is the way, which leadeth unto life, and few there be that find it"* (Matt 7:13-14).

Peter says it is not easy to be saved. *"And, 'If it is hard for the righteous to be saved, what will become of the ungodly and the sinner?'"* (1 Peter 4:18, NIV). We have Biblical precedents of few being saved. Many of us are familiar with some of them.

Noah's family.

Educated guesses and guesstimates of the population before the Flood vary greatly from a few million to several billion. Yet, how many people did God save from the Deluge? 1 Peter 3:20b recalls -- *"the longsuffering of God waited in the days of Noah, while the ark was a preparing, wherein few, that is, eight souls were saved by water."* That is right, only eight persons survived.

Lot and his daughters.

When God destroyed the twin sin-cities of Sodom and Gomorrah, only Lot and his two daughters were able to escape. *"...the men grasped his hand and the hands of his wife and of his two daughters and led them safely out of the city, for the LORD was merciful to them. As soon as they had brought them out, one of them said, 'Flee for your lives! Don't look back, and don't stop anywhere in the plain! Flee to the mountains or you will be swept away!'"* (Gen 19:16b-17, NIV). Lot's wife, though, looked back and was turned into a pillar of salt.

Joshua and Caleb.

Six hundred thousand Israelite men left Egypt in the Exodus. *"And the children of Israel journeyed from Rameses to Succoth, about six hundred thousand on foot that were men, beside children"* (Ex 12:37). Women and children below twenty years of age were not part of the count. If they had been counted, the total would have been around two million.

They displeased God when they shrank back in fear from His instruction to conquer Canaan. *"Surely none of the men that came up out of Egypt, from twenty years old and upward, shall see the land which I sware unto Abraham, unto Isaac, and unto Jacob; because they have not wholly followed me: Save Caleb the son of Jephunneh the Kenezite, and Joshua the son of Nun"* (Num 32:11-12a). Result? After forty years in the wilderness, of the 600,000 men who left Egypt only two lived long enough to enter the Promised Land. (More in the Appendix.)

The chosen people.

Among the numerous peoples of the world, God picked the tiny nation of Israel. *"The LORD did not set his love upon you, nor choose you, because ye were more in number than any people; for ye were the fewest of all people"* (Deut 7:7).

Only Israel, not all nations, was to be saved by the Messiah, as the angel told Joseph. *"And she shall bring forth a son, and thou shalt call his name JESUS: for he shall save his people from their sins"* (Matt 1:21). Christ told the Canaanite woman, *"I was sent only to the lost sheep of Israel"* (Matt 15:24, NIV); and the apostles, *"These twelve Jesus sent forth, and commanded them, saying, Go not into the way of the Gentiles, and into any city of the Samaritans enter ye not: But go rather to the lost sheep of the house of Israel"* (Matt 10:5-6).

Chosen few.

Salvation is not even for all Israel, but for just a chosen few. *"And when he was alone, they that were about him with the twelve asked of him the parable. And he said unto them, Unto you it is given to know the mystery of the kingdom of God: but unto them that are without, all these things are done in parables: That seeing they may see, and not perceive; and hearing they may hear, and not understand; lest at any time they should be converted, and their sins should be forgiven them"* (Mark 4:10-12; cf. Matt 13:10-11; Luke 8:10). Curiously, many of the Jews who came to hear Him were not destined to be saved!

Christ sums up one of His parables, *"For many are called, but few are chosen"* (Matt 22:14; cf. 20:16).

Salvation not for all?

But... is not salvation for all men? Christ had said in John 3:16 -- *"For God so loved the world that he gave his only begotten Son, that whosoever believeth in him should not perish, but have everlasting life."* Indeed, He died on the cross to atone for the sins of all mankind. He repeated the message on many occasions. *"And if any man hear my words, and believe not, I judge him not: for I came not to judge the world, but to save the world"* (John 12:47, etc.).

After Christ ascended to heaven, the apostles harped on His promise. *"And being made perfect, he became the author of eternal salvation unto all them that obey him"* (Heb 5:9, etc.). Note, however, that salvation is premised on obedience.

To obey or not to obey.

God loves the world and wants all men to be saved; that is why He has given us His Son and His word, the Bible, to show us the way that leads to His kingdom and eternal life.

Yet, God has also given each one of us free will – the liberty to do as we please, to choose to obey or disobey. He stressed this through Moses: *"I call heaven and earth to witness against you today, that I have set before you life and death, the blessing and the curse. So choose life in order that you may live, you and your descendants"* (Deut 30:19, NASU).

The problem is, most men choose to disobey – picking the curse over the blessing, death over life. Thus, only the very few who obey will be saved.

God tests men

It was very much the same case with the angels. They all had the gift of free will – to choose between joining Satan and remaining faithful to God. The fallen angels failed the test. It is now us earthly humans whom the LORD is testing to find the worthy replacements for the unfaithful sons of God.

During difficult times, we often hear the seemingly worn-out expression that "God is just testing us." It is actually from several Bible verses. In Psalm 7:9 (NKJV), *"Oh, let the wickedness of the wicked come to an end, But establish the just; For the righteous God tests the hearts and minds."* In Proverbs 17:3 (NKJV), *"The refining pot is for silver and the furnace for gold, But the LORD tests the hearts."* In 1 Thessalonians 2:4-5 (NIV), *"We are not trying to please men but God, who tests our hearts."*

Forty years in the wilderness.

Egypt is just next-door neighbor to Israel, the site of ancient Canaan, the Promised Land. From Rameses in the northeastern section of the Nile Delta to Canaan is just about 250 miles, but it took the Israelites forty years to get there!

Moses, before he died, told them why. *"And thou shalt remember all the way which the LORD thy God led thee these forty years in the wilderness, to humble thee, and to prove thee, to know what was in thine heart, whether thou wouldest keep his commandments, or no"* (Deut 8:2). God made the Israelites "beat around the bush" for forty years in the wilderness -- to see if they would obey His law or not -- before allowing the remnant to enter the Promised Land.

Prophetic "types" and models

Many "types" or prophetic models representing angels are hidden in the Scriptures. Let us uncover as many as we can.

Eliezer, Eleazar, Lazarus, Ezra. We saw earlier that the name of Abraham's servant, Eliezer, can mean "God's helper" and is thus a "type" of the angels. "Eleazar" is a Hebrew variant, while "Lazarus" is the corrupted Latin version. Elliezer without the *Eli* ("God of") becomes "Ezra," which alone means "help" or "helper." The four names typify both the angels and the saints.

First resurrection. In Luke 16:22 (*"And it came to pass, that the beggar died, and was carried by the angels into Abraham's bosom"*), the beggar Lazarus represents the elect who will be gathered by the angels in the first resurrection or Rapture (Matt 24:31) to eventually become "as the angels" in heaven (Matt 22:30; Mark 12:25).

After 4,000 years. In John 11:39 (*"Jesus said, Take ye away the stone. Martha, the sister of him that was dead, saith unto him, Lord, by this time he stinketh: for he hath been dead four days"*), Lazarus (the elect) will be brought back to life after most saints will have been dead for nearly 4,000 years ("four days") since God's first covenant with Abraham.

Millennial Kingdom. In Ezra 7:6a,7b (*"This Ezra went up from Babylon... unto Jerusalem, in the seventh year of Artaxerxes the king"*), Prophetically, it means Ezra (the elect) will leave Babylon (the world) and go to Jerusalem (the Millennial

Kingdom) in the 7th year (the seventh millennium or thousand years from the creation of Adam).

Marriage of the Lamb. In Genesis 24:4 (Abraham told his servant, *"thou shalt go unto my country, and to my kindred, and take a wife unto my son Isaac"*). Abraham is a "type" for God; the servant (Eliezer) personifies the angels whom God will send to fetch the "bride" (the saints) for his son Isaac (Christ, the bridegroom), (Rev 21:9-10.)

Did you notice how the names Lazarus, Ezra, and Eliezer are used synonymously to mean either the saints or the angels as though they are one and the same? It seems to show that the saints will truly become angels.

Pairs and triads

Other prophetic "types" come in pairs and triads. Many illustrate the expulsion of the fallen angels from heaven. When sons are portrayed, the father is a 'type" for God.

Two sons of Adam. As most of us know, Adam's elder son Cain killed his younger brother Abel.

Cain means "weapon-maker" or "acquired." It is quite possible that Cain killed Abel with a weapon he had made.

Abel signifies "breath, vapor"; hence, "spirit." "Son" in Assyrian is *ablu*; in Babylonian, *abil*. Abel is a "type" for Christ, the Only Begotten Son of God (John 1:18, etc.), while Cain is a "type" for Satan, a created son of God (an angel).

Satan killed Christ by inducing the Jews and the Romans to crucify Him (Rev 12:4). As Cain was banished from the presence of the LORD in Eden (Gen 4:14-16), so was Satan expelled from heaven.

Two sons of Abraham. Abram had two sons – the older illegitimate Ishmael, by his wife's maid Hagar; and the younger legitimate Isaac, by his wife Sarah.

Ishmael, was sent away for mocking Isaac (Gen 21:8-14). He is a "type" of the fallen angels, who were cast out of heaven.

Isaac, the younger son who came later, is a "type" of the saints, who will become sons of God later. Like Isaac, they will stay in the house of the Father (kingdom of heaven).

Twin sons of Isaac. The twins Esau and Jacob are likewise "types" illustrating God's master plan of salvation.

Esau, the first one out, was named so ("rough"), because of the roughness of his "hairy" skin (Gen 25:25). He is a "type" of the fallen angels, who have become hairy demons! Psalm 68:21 describes the devil as "hairy." The Hebrew term *sair* ("shaggy") can mean "he-goat," "devil," "faun," or "satyr."

Jacob, second of the twins, had a name meaning "heel-catcher," as he was clutching the heel of Esau when he came out. "Jacob" has come to mean "supplanter" (one who takes the place of another), in the sense of following in the footsteps of a predecessor. Jacob (later renamed Israel) took the place of his older brother for the birthright of the firstborn. He is a "type" of the saints, who will take the place of the fallen angels!

Two sons of Joseph. The eleventh and favorite son of Jacob, Joseph sired two sons, whom *"Asenath the daughter of Poti-pherah priest of On bare unto him"* (Gen 41:50-52).

Manasseh, the firstborn, has a name that means "causing to forget." He is a "type" of the fallen angels, who are destined to be forgotten and relegated to oblivion.

Ephraim, the younger, bears a name signifying "doubly fruitful." He is a "type" of the saints, who will "doubly" bear fruit to God in two groups – as the elect (Israel in the first resurrection) and the rest of the saints (Gentiles in the second resurrection). In much the same way that the younger Ephraim was blessed by Jacob over the older Manasseh (Gen 48:9-20), so will the latecomer saints be blessed over the fallen angels who had been created before them.

Two sons of Moses. After fleeing Egypt, Moses fathered two sons by Zipporah (Ex 18:2-4), daughter of Jethro, priest of Midian (Ex 3:1).

Gershom, the name of the elder, means "outcast, exile," from the root-word *garash* ("to cast out"). Gershom is a "type" of the fallen angels, who have been cast out of heaven.

Eliezer, the younger son, whose name is "God's help or helper," is prophetic of the saints, who will be as the angels in heaven, taking the place of the fallen ones.

Two sisters of Lazarus. When Christ came to raise Lazarus (a "type" of the saints) from the dead, *"Martha, as soon as she heard that Jesus was coming, went and met him: but Mary sat still in the house"* (John 11:20).

Martha is the feminine of *mar* ("lord" in Aramaic) and thus means "lady, mistress" (the lord's wife or bride). That she met Christ on His arrival shows she is a "type" of the elect, who will be caught up to meet Christ in the air as His bride (Rev 21:2,9) in the first resurrection at the Second Coming (1 Thess 4:17).

Mary is the English transliteration of the Greek "Maria" from the Hebrew "Miryam" taken from the root *marah,* meaning "bitter, or rebellious." She is a "type" of those who rebel against God, and will be very bitter when they find themselves outside the kingdom of God (Luke 13:27-28). .

Two goats on Day of Atonement. Each year, on the Day of Atonement, the high priest took two young goats as offerings to God. Chosen by lot, the first goat was killed as a sin-offering to God; the other goat, called the "scapegoat," was driven into the wilderness over a cliff to its death (Lev 16:5,8-10).

The goat for sin-offering is thus a "type" for Christ, who was killed for the sins of mankind. "Scapegoat" is translated from the Hebrew *azazel,* from the root-word *azal,* meaning "to go away, disappear." In the margin of the Revised Version of the Bible, *azazel* is indicated as "removal." *The New Unger's Bible Dictionary* comments: "The most probable rendering of Azazel is 'complete sending away,' i.e., solitude. The rendering then of the passage would be 'the one for Jehovah, and the other for an utter removal.'"[14] The "scapegoat" or *azazel* is a "type" for Satan, who went away and disappeared, completely removed from heaven.

6

Man's Manual for Survival

For this is the love of God, that we keep his commandments: and his commandments are not grievous.

-- 1 John 5:3

Our personal destinies are in our own hands. The Father has shown His love and mercy by telling us how we can each gain eternal life. As it were, He has given us a survival manual. All we have to do now is learn by heart the instructions He has written in it and very carefully follow them.

Dead in sin

To begin with, we are all already dead – spiritually dead, that is. Sin has brought death into the world. *"Therefore, just as sin entered the world through one man, and death through sin, and in this way death came to all men, because all sinned"* (Rom 5:12, NIV). Adam disobeyed God, and his sinful nature has since then passed on to all his descendants, resulting in death.

David lamented in a psalm that he was a sinner even before he was born. *"Behold, I was shapen in iniquity; and in sin did my mother conceive me"* (Ps 51:5). So, all people today, without exception, are sinners. *"For all have sinned, and come short of the glory of God"* (Rom 3:23). Our condition is made worse by the sins we commit in life. *"As for you, you were dead in your transgressions and sins"* (Eph 2:1-2, NIV). And, as if that were not enough, Paul rubs it in. *"And you, being dead in your sins and the uncircumcision of your flesh..."* (Col 2:13a).

Thank God, we can be redeemed from the curse of death through Christ. *"For the wages of sin is death; but the gift of God is eternal life through Jesus Christ our Lord"* (Rom 6:23).

Breaking the law

Paul points out that "sins" can only be considered as such if there are rules defining them as unlawful. *"For until the law sin was in the world: but sin is not imputed when there is no law"* (Rom 5:13). A modern-day analogy is that of pedestrian lanes. If a town does not have any ordinance governing these, people can cross streets anywhere they please without breaking the law. But once the town council issues an ordinance prescribing their use, violators can be arrested and charged with jaywalking.

God handed down His law so men would know what sin is. *"What purpose then does the law serve? It was added because of transgressions..."* (Gal 3:19a, NKJV). So now, with God's commandments, anyone who breaks any of them will know he is committing sin. *"Whosoever committeth sin transgresseth also the law: for sin is the transgression of the law"* (1 John 3:4). Paul adds: *"...by the law is the knowledge of sin"* (Rom 3:20b). And, *"What shall we say then? Is the law sin? Certainly not! On the contrary, I would not have known sin except through the law. For I would not have known covetousness unless the law had said, "You shall not covet."* (Rom 7:7, NKJV).

Key to eternal life.

Keeping the law of God is key to gaining eternal life. *"And, behold, one came and said unto him, Good Master, what good thing shall I do, that I may have eternal life? And he said unto him, Why callest thou me good? there is none good but one, that is, God: but if thou wilt enter into life, keep the commandments"* (Matt 19:16-17). Obeying the commandments of God can spell the difference between spending eternity in the kingdom of heaven and in the lake of fire.

In Christ's depiction of life after death in Luke 16:27-31, the rich man who found himself in torment wanted to spare his brothers from his fate by sending the beggar Lazarus back to warn them. But *"Abraham saith unto him, They have Moses and the prophets; let them hear them. And he said, Nay, father Abraham: but if one went unto them from the dead, they will repent. And he said unto him, If they hear not Moses and the prophets, neither will they be persuaded, though one rose from the dead."* By Moses, Abraham meant the Mosaic law that God gave men through Moses; and by the prophets, he alluded to the teachings of Christ, whose coming the prophets foretold.

In Christ's words, keeping the Mosaic law and having faith in Him go hand-in-hand. *"For had ye believed Moses, ye would have believed me: for he wrote of me. But if ye believe not his writings, how shall ye believe my words?"* (John 5:46-47).

Covenants with God

The law has been handed down through covenants (pacts, agreements or contracts) between God and men. God entered into several covenants with godly men, beginning with Noah after the Flood.

Noahic covenant.

God told Noah, *"And I will establish my covenant with you; neither shall all flesh be cut off any more by the waters of a flood; neither shall there any more be a flood to destroy the earth"* (Gen 9:11); and *"While the earth remaineth, seedtime and harvest, and cold and heat, and summer and winter, and day and night shall not cease"* (Gen 8:22).

In addition to the previous vegetarian diet of men, God gave them all kinds of animal for food: *"Every moving thing that liveth shall be meat for you; even as the green herb have I given you all things"* (Gen 9:3). For their part, men must not eat blood. *"But flesh with the life thereof, which is the blood thereof, shall ye not eat"* (Gen 9:4).

God sealed their covenant by putting the rainbow in the sky. *"And God said, This is the token of the covenant which I make between me and you and every living creature that is with you, for perpetual generations: I do set my bow in the cloud, and it shall be for a token of a covenant between me and the earth"* (Gen 9:12-13). There was no rainbow before the Flood!

Abrahamic covenant.

God made another covenant with Abraham. He promised to bless his descendants as His chosen people if in return Abraham would have faith in Him as God and be the channel of His blessings to the world. *"And I will bless them that bless thee, and curse him that curseth thee: and in thee shall all families of the earth be blessed"* (Gen 12:3), implying that the Messiah who would save the world would come from Abraham.

The Promised Land was to be their reward: *"And I will give unto thee, and to thy seed after thee, the land wherein thou art a stranger, all the land of Canaan, for an everlasting possession; and I will be their God"* (Gen 17:8). The pact was ratified with the establishment of circumcision among all male Hebrews. *"This is my covenant, which ye shall keep, between me and you and thy seed after thee; Every man child among you shall be circumcised"* (Gen 17:10).

Mosaic covenant.

At Mount Sinai, after leaving Egypt in the Exodus, the Israelites affirmed their covenant with God by accepting His law. *"And Moses came and told the people all the words of the LORD, and all the judgments: and all the people answered with one voice, and said, All the words which the LORD hath said will we do"* (Ex 24:3).

They were to be rewarded with God's protection, prosperity, victory over enemies, and the outpouring of His Spirit on them (Ex 23:20-33). Circumcision remained the seal of the covenant. *"Speak unto the children of Israel, saying, If a woman have conceived seed, and born a man child... in the eighth day the flesh of his foreskin shall be circumcised"* (Lev 12:2a,3).

God repeated the prohibition he told Noah on eating blood. *"For the life of the flesh is in the blood: and I have given it to you upon the altar to make an atonement for your souls: for it is the blood that maketh an atonement for the soul"* (Lev 17:10-11). For this reason, animal sacrifice as substitute payment for sin became a main feature of the Mosaic law.

Davidic covenant.
God established David and his descendants as kings on the throne of Israel. Moreover, *"And when thy days be fulfilled, and thou shalt sleep with thy fathers, I will set up thy seed after thee, which shall proceed out of thy bowels, and I will establish his kingdom"* (2 Sam 7:12). The future king would be the promised Messiah, who would come from the house of David.

The prophecy was fulfilled when Christ, a descendant of David, was born in Bethlehem about a thousand years after God made the promise to David.

The new covenant.
God had promised a new covenant to His chosen people. *"Behold, the days come, saith the LORD, that I will make a new covenant with the house of Israel, and with the house of Judah: Not according to the covenant that I made with their fathers in the day that I took them by the hand to bring them out of the land of Egypt; which my covenant they brake, although I was an husband unto them, saith the LORD: But this shall be the covenant that I will make with the house of Israel; After those days, saith the LORD, I will put my law in their inward parts, and write it in their hearts; and will be their God, and they shall be my people"* (Jer 31:31-33).

Christ's death on the cross established the new covenant, doing away with animal sacrifices and the Temple priesthood. In Hebrews 8:6b, He is referred to as *"the mediator of a better covenant, which was established upon better promises."* He is "*an high priest of good things to come,*" of "*a greater and more perfect tabernacle.*" In other words, Christ is now our high priest in the tabernacle or Temple in heaven.

Blood of Christ. Whereas the blood of animal sacrifices "*repeated endlessly year after year*" made for ceremonial cleansing only and "*can never... make perfect*" or "*cleanse us from a guilty conscience*" (Heb 10:1,22, NIV), Christ "*entered the Most Holy Place once for all by his own blood, having obtained eternal redemption*" for us (Heb 9:12, NIV). The new covenant, through the blood of Christ shed "*once for all,*" achieved what the old covenant could not with repetitious sacrifices – the cleansing of the conscience.

God's law abolished?

In Paul's writings, specially in his epistle to the Romans, some passages look like they say that God's commandments need no longer be observed, with Christ as the reason: *"For Christ is the end of the law for righteousness to every one that believeth"* (Rom 10:4). It is now the grace of God that saves us. *"For sin shall not have dominion over you: for ye are not under the law, but under grace"* (Rom 6:14).

Paul seems to say that there is no salvation in the law: *"Therefore by the deeds of the law there shall no flesh be justified in his sight"* (Rom 3:20a). He adds that, when we become members of the body of Christ, we die to the law and are released from it. *"But now we are delivered from the law, that being dead wherein we were held; that we should serve in newness of spirit, and not in the oldness of the letter"* (Rom 7:6).

The law upheld.

However, Paul himself says the law is still in force! *"Do we then make void the law through faith? God forbid: yea, we establish the law"* (Rom 3:31). The people whom God finds acceptable are those who obey the law. *"For not the hearers of the law are just before God, but the doers of the law shall be justified"* (Rom 2:13). Is Paul contradicting himself? Is he guilty of doublespeak – saying one thing and meaning another?

Tough topics. Peter notes that *"our beloved brother Paul also according to the wisdom given unto him hath written unto you; As also in all his epistles, speaking in them of these things; in which are some things hard to be understood, which they that are unlearned and unstable wrest, as they do also the other scriptures, unto their own destruction"* (2 Peter 3:15a-16). Some of the things Paul wrote about are hard to understand!

Unchanging validity.

Christ affirmed the continuing validity of the Mosaic law. *"Think not that I am come to destroy the law, or the prophets: I am not come to destroy, but to fulfil. For verily I say unto you, Till heaven and earth pass, one jot or one tittle shall in no wise pass from the law, till all be fulfilled"* (Matt 5:17-18). The law will remain unchanged until all prophecies shall have come to pass.

The new covenant did not take the old out of the way. *"In that he saith, A new covenant, he hath made the first old. Now that which decayeth and waxeth old is ready to vanish away"* (Heb 8:13). The old covenant is nearly obsolete, but it is still in place. For instance, God had said that "*it is the blood that maketh an atonement for the soul"* (Lev 17:11). It still does; the law has not changed – only now it is the blood of Christ, and not the blood of animals, that atones for the sins of men.

Severe sentences lightened.
So, why did Paul say that we are no longer under the law? He gives us some inkling in Colossians 2:14, which says Christ blotted *"out the handwriting of ordinances that was against us, which was contrary to us, and took it out of the way, nailing it to his cross."* It sounds like some portions of the law were harsh, but Christ has made them less severe for us.

We get more hints from Romans 8:2 -- *"For the law of the Spirit of life in Christ Jesus hath made me free from the law of sin and death."* Fausset's Bible Dictionary explains that the law "convicted of sin and was therefore '*a ministration of condemnation*' and '*of death...*' (2 Cor 3:7,9)."[1]

Indeed, many transgressions of the Mosaic law condemn the violators to death. Christ's love, however, has softened the severity of the law, as we see in some New Testament incidents.

The adulteress. In John 8:3-11, the scribes and Pharisees caught a woman in the act of adultery, but, before stoning her to death as the law prescribed (Deut 22:22), they brought her to Christ. *"So when they continued asking him, he lifted up himself, and said unto them, He that is without sin among you, let him first cast a stone at her... And they which heard it, being convicted by their own conscience, went out one by one, beginning at the eldest, even unto the last: and Jesus was left alone, and the woman standing in the midst. When Jesus had lifted up himself, and saw none but the woman, he said unto her, Woman, where are those thine accusers? hath no man condemned thee? She said, No man, Lord. And Jesus said unto her, Neither do I condemn thee: go, and sin no more."*

Adultery is still a sin; but Christ forgave the woman, thus saving her from the condemnation of death.

The eunuch. Under the law, *"No one who is emasculated or has his male organ cut off shall enter the assembly of the LORD"* (Deut 23:1, NASU).

Yet, in Acts 8:36-38, the evangelist Philip baptized a eunuch from Ethiopia. *"And as they went on their way, they came unto a certain water: and the eunuch said, See, here is water; what doth hinder me to be baptized? And Philip said, If thou believest with all thine heart, thou mayest. And he answered and said, I believe that Jesus Christ is the Son of God. And he commanded the chariot to stand still: and they went down both into the water, both Philip and the eunuch; and he baptized him."*

Paul preached the idea. *"There is neither Jew nor Greek, there is neither bond nor free, there is neither male nor female: for ye are all one in Christ Jesus"* (Gal 3:28; cf. Col 3:11).

The Ten Commandments

God gave the written law to Moses at Mount Sinai as the Israelites headed for the Promised Land from Egypt. *"And he gave unto Moses, when he had made an end of communing with him upon mount Sinai, two tables of testimony, tables of stone, written with the finger of God"* (Ex 31:18). God Himself wrote the commandments on the two stone tablets.

Decalogue.

The Ten Commandments are also called the "Decalogue," from the Greek words *deka* ("ten") and *logos* ("word"). The term was "first found in Clement of Alexandria's Pedag.iii. 12."[2]

The set of instructions is found in two places in the Old Testament: in Exodus 20:2-17, as given by God to Moses word-for-word; and in Deuteronomy 5:6-21, as retold by Moses, with a slight difference in wording.

Various versions

The Ten Commandments are not numbered in the original text, so there have been variations in the division of verses. Jewish historian Josephus (37-100 AD) was the first to write about the arrangement now common among Protestants (except Lutherans), with the following order: I. one God (vv. 2-3); II. images (vv. 4-6); III. name of God (v. 7); IV. seventh-day

Sabbath (vv. 8-11); V. parents (v.12); VI. murder (v. 13); VII. adultery (v. 14); VIII. theft (v. 15); IX. false witness (v. 16); X. coveting (v. 17).[3]

Three other commonly known versions of the Decalogue, divided to conform to the beliefs or doctrines of the respective religions or denominations teaching them, are the Philonic, Augustinian, and Talmudic.

Philonic. Before Josephus, Jewish philosopher Philo of Alexandria (15 BC-50 AD) made the same division, except that he followed the Septuagint (Greek translation of the Hebrew scriptures) in putting adultery before murder. This mode of counting was used by many of the church Fathers, and is now prevalent in the Greek Orthodox and most Protestant churches.[4]

Augustinian. Advocated by Saint Augustine (354-430 AD), one of the leaders of the early Christian church, this version combines other gods and images (Ex 20:3-6) into the first commandment. Roman Catholicism adopted this mode, which dilutes the prohibition on the use of images.[5]

To maintain the number of ten, this method divides and follows the order of Deuteronomy 5:21, which makes the prohibition of coveting a neighbor's wife the 9th, and coveting his house and other possessions the 10th.

Roman Catholics and Lutherans accept Augustine's mode of reckoning, except that they follow the order in Exodus 20:17, so that the 9th commandment forbids the coveting of a neighbor's house, while the 10th names his wife and other properties.[6]

Talmudic. This version was adopted by the Jews in the early centuries of the Christian era and became the standard among them in the Middle Ages up to the present time. Accordingly, Exodus 20:2 (which is not really a commandment, but a declaration) appears as the "first word" of the Decalogue.

Exodus 20:3-6 became the second commandment, while the following eight commandments are the same as in the common Protestant arrangement.[7]

(Please see the table on the next page. On the left of the table, the Roman numerals indicate the division as recorded by Josephus. The three columns on the right with Arabic numerals show how the Decalogue is divided by the Protestants/Philonic, Catholics/Augustinian, and Jews/Talmudic, respectively.)

Various Decalogue Numberings*

Exodus 20:2-17	P[1]	A[2]	T[3]
I. *2 I am the LORD thy God, which have brought thee out of the land of Egypt, out of the house of bondage.*	1		1
3 Thou shalt have no other gods before me.	1	1	2
II. *4 Thou shalt not make unto thee any graven image, or any likeness of any thing that is in heaven above, or that is in the earth beneath, or that is in the water under the earth:*	2	1	2
5 Thou shalt not bow down thyself to them, nor serve them: for I the LORD thy God am a jealous God, visiting the iniquity of the fathers upon the children unto the third and fourth generation of them that hate me;	2	1	2
6 And shewing mercy unto thousands of them that love me, and keep my commandments.	2	1	2
III. *7 Thou shalt not take the name of the LORD thy God in vain; for the LORD will not hold him guiltless that taketh his name in vain.*	3	2	3
IV. *8 Remember the sabbath day, to keep it holy.*	4	3	4
9 Six days shalt thou labour, and do all thy work:	4	3	4
10 But the seventh day is the sabbath of the LORD thy God: in it thou shalt not do any work, thou, nor thy son, nor thy daughter, thy manservant, nor thy maidservant, nor thy cattle, nor thy stranger that is within thy gates:	4	3	4
11 For in six days the LORD made heaven and earth, the sea, and all that in them is, and rested the seventh day: wherefore the LORD blessed the sabbath day, and hallowed it.	4	3	4
V. *12 Honour thy father and thy mother: that thy days may be long upon the land which the LORD thy God giveth thee.*	5	4	5
VI. *13 Thou shalt not kill.*	7	5	6
VII. *14 Thou shalt not commit adultery.*	6	6	7
VIII. *15 Thou shalt not steal.*	8	7	8
IX. *16 Thou shalt not bear false witness against thy neighbour.*	9	8	9
X. *17a Thou shalt not covet thy neighbour's house,*	10	10	10
17b thou shalt not covet thy neighbour's wife,	10	9	10
17c nor his manservant, nor his maidservant, nor his ox, nor his ass, nor any thing that is thy neighbour's.	10	10	10

*Roman numerals, per Josephus; [1] Philonic; [2] Augustinian; [3] Talmudic

Revisions. Some churches have gone so far as to change or delete parts of the Decalogue as originally written in Scriptures. They are in danger of the judgment pronounced in Revelation 22:18-19 -- *"For I testify unto every man that heareth the words of the prophecy of this book, If any man shall add unto these things, God shall add unto him the plagues that are written in this book: And if any man shall take away from the words of the book of this prophecy, God shall take away his part out of the book of life, and out of the holy city, and from the things which are written in this book."*

Though found only in the book of Revelation, the passage, according to some Bible commentators, serves as an epilogue for the entire Bible, both Old and New Testaments. So, beware.

Three for God's chosen people.

Of the Ten Commandments, three (I, II, and IV) were specially for Israel. In fact, God introduces Himself as *"I am the LORD thy God, which have brought thee out of the land of Egypt"* (Ex 20:2a), "the LORD" being a substitute for God's personal name "YHWH" in the original text.

As the Israelites were surrounded by nations of polytheists and idolaters whom they might be tempted to follow, I and II specify the worship of the one true God "YHWH" and the rejection of graven images. As for IV, resting on the seventh day, they must have been prone to forget what they already knew, as the verse begins with the word *"Remember..."* (Ex 20:8).

Aliens included. Foreigners in Israel come under the law. *"One ordinance shall be both for you of the congregation, and also for the stranger that sojourneth with you, an ordinance for ever in your generations: as ye are, so shall the stranger be before the LORD"* (Num 15:15). Additionally, *"The same laws and regulations will apply both to you and to the alien living among you"* (Num 15:16, NIV).

Seven in the conscience.

Seven commandments were apparently universal in the consciences of ancient men even before the time of Moses -- murder, adultery, theft and false witness were already punished as crimes among the Babylonians and the Egyptians; and to profane God's name, disrespect one's parents, and covet the property of another were obviously wrong to most people.[8]

Paul confirms this in Romans 2:14-15 -- *"For when the Gentiles, which have not the law, do by nature the things contained in the law, these, having not the law, are a law unto themselves: Which shew the work of the law written in their hearts, their conscience also bearing witness, and their thoughts the mean while accusing or else excusing one another."*

One in the mind.

The first nine commandments involve action or speech that can be perceived by other people. But the tenth (coveting) is known only to the person and God. Evidently, we can sin not only physically or orally, but mentally as well.

Mental sins. By just thinking of, say, killing someone, we have already committed murder! Christ and John give us some examples. In Matt 5:28 -- *"But I say unto you, That whosoever looketh on a woman to lust after her hath committed adultery with her already in his heart."* And in 1 John 3:15 -- *"Whosoever hateth his brother is a murderer: and ye know that no murderer hath eternal life abiding in him."*

Four only for Gentiles?

As many new converts were baptized, questions arose as to whether Gentile converts should follow all the commandments the Jews kept. It was brought to the attention of the Council in Jerusalem that *"certain men which came down from Judaea taught the brethren, and said, Except ye be circumcised after the manner of Moses, ye cannot be saved"* (Acts 15:1a).

After much discussion, James, the council leader, decided: *"Wherefore my sentence is, that we trouble not them, which from among the Gentiles are turned to God: But that we write unto them, that... ye abstain from meats offered to idols, and from blood, and from things strangled, and from fornication: from which if ye keep yourselves, ye shall do well"* (Acts 15:19-20a, 29b). The commandments were reduced to four?

Because of that decision, some people mistakenly conclude that the other commandments have been abolished. Yet, if we study the matter closely, we will realize that only those commandments that were most frequently violated at the time were expressly forbidden.

Meats offered to idols. Often meat sacrificed in pagan temples to idols were sold in the marketplaces or served at feasts. Eating any such meat would have been tantamount to taking part in the worship of the pagan gods and goddesses.[9,10]

Blood. The eating of blood, again, is strictly forbidden by God. *"For it is the life of all flesh; the blood of it is for the life thereof: therefore I said unto the children of Israel, Ye shall eat the blood of no manner of flesh: for the life of all flesh is the blood thereof: whosoever eateth it shall be cut off"* (Lev 17:14).

Things strangled. "Such meat was considered a delicacy by many pagans."[11] Animals and fowl were strangled or beaten before cooking without bloodletting. The prohibition includes those caught or killed by hunters. *"Any Israelite or any alien living among you who hunts any animal or bird that may be eaten must drain out the blood and cover it with earth"* (Lev 17:13, NIV).

Fornication. The ruling by the Jerusalem Council might have referred to immorality in general or to religious prostitution in pagan temples.[12] Sexual intercourse with a partner other than one's spouse was not considered disgraceful by many ancient peoples. "It was practiced without shame and remorse."[13]

Others not mentioned.

Commandments whose observance was taken for granted, but were not mentioned by the Jerusalem Council, remain in force. For example, love of God, honoring His name and respect for our parents were presumed. Sabbath-keeping was a regular practice, inasmuch as Christianity began as a sect of the Jews. Murder, theft, and false witness were punishable by law.

Ark of the covenant

After giving Moses the Decalogue on the two tablets of stone, God told Moses to make a wooden chest. *"And they shall make an ark of shittim wood… And thou shalt make a mercy seat… And thou shalt put the mercy seat above upon the ark; and in the ark thou shalt put the testimony that I shall give thee. And there I will meet with thee, and I will commune with thee from above the mercy seat, from between the two cherubims which are upon the ark of the testimony, of all things which I will give thee in commandment unto the children of Israel"* (Ex 25:10a,17a,21-22). God was to give Moses more commandments for Israel from above the ark of the testimony or covenant.

613 commandments

In time, the additional commandments God gave to Moses totaled 613 (including the first ten on the two tablets of stone). These consist of 248 instructions and 365 prohibitions.

According to author Chuck Missler (*Cosmic Codes*, revised 2004), the commandments were given over a period of fifty days – from the first in Egypt (on Passover) until the 613th (on the Feast of Weeks or Pentecost) in Sinai.[14]

Author Grant Jeffrey (*The Signature of God*, 1996) reports a Jewish tradition that Moses copied the other parts from black letters of fire he saw against a background of white flame.[15] It seems hinted at in Deuteronomy 33:2. *"And he said, The LORD came from Sinai, and rose up from Seir unto them; he shined forth from mount Paran, and he came with ten thousands of saints: from his right hand went a fiery law for them."*

The outline of the Mosaic law is in Exodus chapters 20-23.[16] Some scholars refer to Leviticus chapters 17-26 as the "holiness code."[17] Most of the 613 commandments are here. Do you think they are too many as to be impossible to keep? Not really.

Five divisions.

The great 12th century Jewish philosopher Maimonides, in his most important work, the Misnah Torah, codified the 613 commandments under various headings. These can be further subdivided into five groups. In this way, we can more easily tell which commandments are still in force, optional, suspended, or have been substituted for. The five divisions are as follows:

1. Worship law (love of God)
2. Moral law (love of fellow creatures)
3. National law (to set Israel apart from other nations)
4. Civil law (for the theocratic governance of Israel)
5. Ceremonial law (for Temple priests and offerings)

Two groupings.
The five divisions can further be reduced to two groups as Christ taught: *"Whosoever therefore shall break one of these least commandments, and shall teach men so, he shall be called the least in the kingdom of heaven: but whosoever shall do and teach them, the same shall be called great in the kingdom of heaven"* (Matt 5:19).

We have discussed in the previous chapter what the passage teaches: There are "least" commandments and there are "great" commandments. The "least" commandments are minor and optional, while the "great" commandments are major and compulsory. Now, how can we tell which ones are which?

Defined by Christ. Christ clearly pointed out what the great commandments are in Matthew 22:36-40 when a disciple asked, *"Master, which is the great commandment in the law? Jesus said unto him, Thou shalt love the Lord thy God with all thy heart, and with all thy soul, and with all thy mind. This is the first and great commandment. And the second is like unto it, Thou shalt love thy neighbor as thyself. On these two commandments hang all the law and the prophets."*

The first and second "great" commandments actually make up the Decalogue. The first four command love of God (I. one God "; II. images; III. name of God; IV. seventh-day Sabbath), thus constituting what we may call "worship law"; while the last six exhort love of fellowmen (V. parents; VI. murder; VII. adultery; VIII. theft; IX. false witness; X. coveting), hence making up what is known as "moral law."

The three other divisions, therefore, do not form part of the "great" commandments; they fall under the category of "least commandments" and, as such, are either optional, suspended, or substituted for. Below is how the two groupings appear:

    A. "Great" Commandments
        1. Worship law
        2. Moral law
    B. "Least" Commandments
        3. National law
        4. Civil law
        5. Ceremonial law

The first and second divisions, "worship law" and "moral law," are mandatory. Some of the commandments, though, are repetitive.

The third division, "national law" (for the nation of Israel only -- to set them apart from the many pagan nations around them), is optional or discretionary for Gentiles.

The fourth division, "civil law" (specially for the theocratic governance of Israel), is suspended, because the theocracy (i.e., government headed by God) is not in place in Israel today.

The fifth division, "ceremonial law" (for Temple priests and offerings), has been substituted – with Christ, the Lamb of God (John 1:29,36), now our high priest in heaven (Heb 4:14,8:1, etc.); whose blood has replaced that of sacrificial animals for the atonement of sin (Heb 9:12-14), with the saints now the temple of the Holy Spirit on earth (1 Cor 3:16: 2 Cor 6:16).

Most violated commandments.

Oddly, two great commandments for which God used the most words are the two most misunderstood… and most widely violated. These are the second and fourth commandments.

Second commandment

The second "word" in the Decalogue is the prohibition against the making and worship of graven images (Ex 20:4-6).

A sect sans images.

The first Christians were Jews and Gentile converts who avoided images like the plague. In fact, Christianity was initially regarded as a sect of the Jews. When the high priest and elders accused Paul before the Roman governor, they said: *"For we have found this man a pestilent fellow, and a mover of sedition among all the Jews throughout the world, and a ringleader of the sect of the Nazarenes"* (Acts 24:5).

In Rome, the Jewish leaders told Paul, *"But we desire to hear of thee what thou thinkest: for as concerning this sect, we know that every where it is spoken against"* (Acts 28:22).

Thus, for over three hundred fifty years after the crucifixion, the early Christians, being initially Jewish in worship, made no use of images, even that of Christ.

Images sneaked in.
After almost 300 years of persecution, Christianity was legitimized in 312 AD by Emperor Constantine, who defeated his rival under a banner with the cross. In 380, Emperor Theodosius, outlawed paganism and, in 392, made Christianity the official religion of the Roman Empire. Pagans flocked into the Church, bringing with them their religious customs. Statues and images of pagan gods and goddesses were renamed and called "saints." "Through the centuries, more and more statues were made, until today there are churches in Europe which contain as many as two, three, and four *thousand* statues."[18]

Iconoclastic controversy.
The advocates of icon veneration – "iconophiles" (Greek *eikon*, "image" + *philos*, "lover") – reasoned that, since God had taken a physical form in the person of Christ, He could be portrayed in images. Additionally, the icons served as mediums of instruction for the uneducated.[19] On the other hand, Christians known as iconoclasts (*eikon* + *klaein*, "to break") opposed the use of icons, which they deemed idolatrous. The dispute called the "Iconoclastic Controversy" raged between the two sides.

Images banned, restored. In 725 and 726, Byzantine Emperor Leo III prohibited the worship of images and ordered their destruction. In 730, their use was officially prohibited.[20] The ban was condemned by the pope (who had images in Rome), but the iconoclastic doctrine was rigorously enforced in Constantinople (present-day Istanbul). Leo's son and successor Constantine V also had the worship of images condemned as idolatry at the church council held in Hieria in 754.[21]

In 787, Empress Irene of the East reestablished the use of images at the Second Council of Nicaea, which ordered the restoration of images in churches all over the Roman Empire.[22] In 815, Emperor Leo V again prohibited the use of icons in another church council.[23]

In 843, the pro-icon monk Methodius was elected patriarch and restored icon veneration at the Council of Orthodoxy. The restoration is celebrated annually in the Eastern Church as the Triumph of Orthodoxy.[24]

Fourth commandment

The first Christians kept the fourth commandment religiously – not working or even cooking on Saturday. *"Do not light a fire in any of your dwellings on the Sabbath day"* (Ex 35:3, NIV).

Sabbath abolished?

On several occasions, Christ and His disciples appeared to have broken the seventh day rest-day Sabbath law.

Food-gathering on Sabbath. We read in Mattew 12:1-4, *"At that time Jesus went on the sabbath day through the corn; and his disciples were an hungred, and began to pluck the ears of corn, and to eat. But when the Pharisees saw it, they said unto him, Behold, thy disciples do that which is not lawful to do upon the sabbath day. But he said unto them, Have ye not read what David did, when he was an hungred, and they that were with him; How he entered into the house of God, and did eat the shewbread, which was not lawful for him to eat, neither for them which were with him, but only for the priests?"*

Healing on Sabbath. Christ healed afflicted people in several instances on the Sabbath. *"And, behold, there was a man which had his hand withered. And they asked him, saying, Is it lawful to heal on the sabbath days? That they might accuse him. And he said unto them, What man shall there be among you, that shall have one sheep, and if it fall into a pit on the sabbath day, will he not lay hold on it, and lift it out? How much then is a man better than a sheep? Wherefore it is lawful to do well on the sabbath days."* (Matt 12:10-12; cf. Luke 13:14-16,14:2-4; John 5:10-11).

"And he said unto them, The Sabbath was made for man, and not man for the Sabbath" (Mark 2:27). To paraphrase, God gave the Sabbath to man for his benefit. Should there be a conflict between the Sabbath and pressing necessities for life that cannot be postponed, man's interest can be given priority.

Evidently, the law of the Sabbath is flexible, unlike the other great commandments, which cannot be changed.

Rest day changed.

In 321 AD, to unite the two dominant groups of people in the Roman Empire – pagan sun-worshippers and Christians –

Constantine decreed as the Roman day of rest Sun-Day (day of the sun-god), which Christians also venerated as the day of the Resurrection. The bishops of the Church, who wanted to distance themselves from the Sabbath-keeping Jews, whom they often called "Christ-killers," welcomed the imperial decree.

Pope Sylvester, the bishop of Rome (314-335), subsequently declared Sunday as "the Lord's Day."

In 364, the Council of Laodicea conferred upon Sunday, the first day of the week, the holiness of the seventh-day Sabbath.

Fulfilled prophecy. Thus was fulfilled the prophet's vision in Daniel 7:25a – *"And he shall speak great words against the most High, and shall wear out the saints of the most High, and think to change times and laws."* Rome changed the time or day of the weekly Sabbath, as well as the law against worshipping graven images.

Retained by Reformists. In the 16th century, when Martin Luther, followed by John Calvin and others, led and spread the Reformation, the many Protestant churches that grew out of the movement continued to observe Sunday as the Sabbath day of rest, as well as various other holidays instituted by the Roman Catholic Church that they had broken away from.

Rewards for Sabbath-keeping.

God promises honors to the faithful resting on the seventh day. *"If thou turn away thy foot from the sabbath, from doing thy pleasure on my holy day; and call the sabbath a delight, the holy of the LORD, honourable; and shalt honour him, not doing thine own ways, nor finding thine own pleasure, nor speaking thine own words: Then shalt thou delight thyself in the LORD; and I will cause thee to ride upon the high places of the earth, and feed thee with the heritage of Jacob thy father: for the mouth of the LORD hath spoken it"* (Isa 58:13-14).

He will take them to His house as His children. *"Even unto them will I give in mine house and within my walls a place and a name better than of sons and of daughters: I will give them an everlasting name, that shall not be cut off. Also the sons of the stranger, that join themselves to the LORD, to serve him, and to love the name of the LORD, to be his servants, every one that keepeth the sabbath from polluting it, and taketh hold of my* covenant; *Even them will I bring to my holy mountain, and make them joyful in my house of prayer: their burnt offerings and their sacrifices shall be accepted upon mine altar; for mine house shall be called an house of prayer for all people"* (Isa 56:5-7).

Some "worship law" additions

Several additional commandments that fall under "worship law" (love of God) expand on the first four in the Decalogue.

***Shema*, ("hear").** The believer's confession of faith: *"Hear, O Israel: The LORD our God is one LORD: And thou shalt love the LORD thy God with all thine heart, and with all thy soul, and with all thy might. And these words, which I command thee this day, shall be in thine heart: And thou shalt teach them diligently unto thy children, and shalt talk of them when thou sittest in thine house, and when thou walkest by the way, and when thou liest down, and when thou risest up"* (Deut 6:4-7; full text is in Deut 6:4-9, 11:13-21, and Num 15:37-41). The *Shema* stresses the uniqueness of "YHWH" and the importance of loving Him..

At least the first two verses (Deut 6:4-5; paraphrased in Matt 22:37 and Mark 12:28-30 by Christ) should be recited twice each day, before bedtime and upon waking up.

"Phylacteries" (*tefillin*). The second part of the *Shema* commands wearing the verses literally, *"And thou shalt bind them for a sign upon thine hand, and they shall be as frontlets between thine eyes.* (Deut 6:8).

Male Jews obey by wearing phylacteries (*tefillin*, "prayers") -- small, square leather boxes containing the *Shema* and strapped to their foreheads and left arms. These are worn during weekday morning prayers, but not on Sabbaths or festivals.

***Mezuzah* ("doorpost").** The third part gives the command: *"And thou shalt write them upon the door posts of thine house, and upon thy gates"* (Deut 6:9, 11:20) -- to continually remind Israel of their obligations to God.

Observant Jews comply by affixing the *mezuzah*, a small wooden, metal, or glass case containing Deuteronomy 6:4-9 and 11:13-21 on the doorposts of the entrances to their homes.

The fourth part (Deut 11:13-17) promises either blessings or punishments, according to one's obedience to God.

"**Fringes**" ("**tassels**," *tzittzit*). The fifth part commands "*fringes in the borders of their garments*" with "*a ribband of blue*" as a reminder of God's laws (Num 15:38-39). In Deut 22:12, "fringes" is *gedilim* (sing. *gedil*, "twisted thread"); "borders" (*kanpey*, "corners"); "blue" (*tekheleth*, "violet"), but due to uncertainty of the exact meaning, dark blue is used.[25]

Thus, tassels of twisted threads, each with one of deep blue,[26] signifying the heavenly origin of the commandments, are attached to each corner of a rectangular prayer shawl called *tallith*, worn during morning prayers.[27]

Pagan practices prohibited.
God commanded His people to shun pagan practices and cultic customs. *"Do not practice divination or sorcery"* (Lev 19:26b, NIV). *"Do not turn to mediums or seek out spiritists, for you will be defiled by them"* (Lev 19:31a, NIV). *"There shall not be found among you any one that maketh his son or his daughter to pass through the fire, or that useth divination, or an observer of times, or an enchanter, or a witch, Or a charmer, or a consulter with familiar spirits, or a wizard, or a necromancer. For all that do these things are an abomination unto the LORD"* (Deut 18:10-12a).

"Moral law" illustrations

Some of the additional commandments that form part of the 613 fall under "moral law" (love of fellow creatures).

Blood not to be eaten. This strict prohibition was given three times: to Noah (Gen 9:3-4) and to Moses (Lev 7:26, 19:26a) by God; and to the first Gentile converts to Christianity by the Jerusalem Council (Acts 15:29).

Kindness to animals. The Israelites were allowed to eat certain "clean" wild animals and birds, as well as take their young and eggs, but they were to let the mother live (Deut 22:6-7). They were also cautioned, *"Do not cook a young goat in its mother's milk"* (Deut 14:21a, NIV).

Work animals are to be fed adequately to give them the strength they need for doing their work (Deut 25:4). *"Do not plow with an ox and a donkey yoked together"* (Deut 22:10, NIV). If one sees the ass of his enemy fall under its load, he must help pull the animal up (Ex 23:5). Beasts of burden are also to be rested on the Sabbath (Ex 20:8-11; 23:12; Deut 22:1-4).

Sexual perversions. Sodomy and bestiality are extremely detestable to God. *"You shall not lie with a male as with a woman. It is an abomination"* (Lev 18:22, NKJV). *"Nor shall you mate with any animal, to defile yourself with it. Nor shall any woman stand before an animal to mate with it. It is perversion"* (Lev 18:23, NKJV).

Related to these, cross-dressing to masquerade as a member of the opposite sex is also condemned. *"A woman shall not wear anything that pertains to a man, nor shall a man put on a woman's garment, for all who do so are an abomination to the LORD your God"* (Deut 22:5, NKJV).

In the New Testament, Paul observes: *"God gave them up unto vile affections: for even their women did change the natural use into that which is against nature"* (Rom 1:26).

"National law" foundations

This third division of commandments is exclusively for Israel to separate them from the pagan peoples around them. *"You are to be holy to me because I, the LORD, am holy, and I have set you apart from the nations to be my own"* (Lev 20:26, NIV).

Circumcision.

God gave the commandment twice. First to Abraham: *"And he that is eight days old shall be circumcised among you, every man child in your generations, he that is born in the house, or bought with money of any stranger, which is not of thy seed"* (Gen 17:12); and again to Moses: *"If a woman have conceived seed, and born a man child... in the eighth day the flesh of his foreskin shall be circumcised"* (Lev 12:2b,3). It was to be done on the eighth day from birth, and has been so done since.

"Clean" and "unclean" food.

After the Flood, God told Noah men could eat any "moving thing" without distinction (Gen 9:3). In the Mosaic law, however, God divided four-footed animals, fish, birds, and insects into two distinct classes – the "clean" and "unclean" (Lev 11; Acts 10:9-15). Only the "clean" may be used for food by the Israelites.

Four-footed animals. Those that chew the cud and have parted hooves, like cattle and sheep, are "clean" (Lev 11:3,4,7). Pigs, which have divided hooves, but do not chew the cud, are "unclean." Camels and horses chew the cud, but do not have split hooves, so they cannot be eaten, either. Camel's milk and cheese made from it, though, are not forbidden.

Water creatures. Fish with fins and scales are fit for food (Lev 11:9-1). *"Whatsoever hath no fins nor scales in the waters, that shall be an abomination unto you"* (Lev 11:12). Hence, eels and catfish, and shellfish like shrimps, crabs, clams, and oysters, as well as squids and octopuses, are all "unclean."

Birds. Twenty different species of birds were named as unfit for food (11:13-19). These were mostly predators and carrion-eaters. Not mentioned and thus presumed "clean" are fowl in the likes of the quail, pigeon, chicken, turkey, duck, goose, etc., which mainly feed on grains, plants, insects, and invertebrates.

Insects. Insects, in general, and flying insects, in particular, are taboo. *"There are, however, some winged creatures that walk on all fours that you may eat: those that have jointed legs for hopping on the ground. Of these you may eat any kind of locust, katydid, cricket or grasshopper"* (Lev 11:21, NIV).

"Creeping things." Reptiles, amphibians, and burrowing animals are all unfit for food. *"And every creeping thing that creeps on the earth shall be an abomination. It shall not be eaten. Whatever crawls on its belly, whatever goes on all fours, or whatever has many feet among all creeping things that creep on the earth -- these you shall not eat, for they are an abomination"* (Lev 11:41-42, NKJV).

Dead animals. Whatever the cause of death, dead animals are a no-no. *"Do not eat anything you find already dead. You may give it to an alien living in any of your towns, and he may eat it, or you may sell it to a foreigner. But you are a people holy to the LORD your God"* (Deut 14:21, NIV).

Confirmed by science.

The wisdom of the Mosaic law is only now being confirmed by modern science. The eighth day from birth is perfect for circumcision, because the levels of Vitamin K and prothrombin, both blood-clotting factors, are highest at this time in life.

Pork may harbor parasites that can be passed on to people. Shellfish, scale-less fish, most insects and many reptiles are scavengers. Mollusks and crustaceans spoil quickly in hot weather. Some birds feed on dead bodies, which can, needless to say, spawn diseases, even epidemics.

Declared "clean" by Christ.
Christ nonetheless suggested that it was permissible to eat "unclean" foods. *"Are you so dull?" he asked. 'Don't you see that nothing that enters a man from the outside can make him `unclean'? For it doesn't go into his heart but into his stomach, and then out of his body.' (In saying this, Jesus declared all foods 'clean.') He went on: 'What comes out of a man is what makes him `unclean.' For from within, out of men's hearts, come evil thoughts, sexual immorality, theft, murder, adultery, greed, malice, deceit, lewdness, envy, slander, arrogance and folly. All these evils come from inside and make a man `unclean'"* (Mark 7:18-23, NIV; cf. Matt 15;16-20).

Seen by the apostles. Peter had a vision of a great sheet lowered from heaven with *"all kinds of four-footed animals, as well as reptiles of the earth and birds of the air. Then a voice told him, 'Get up, Peter. Kill and eat.' 'Surely not, Lord!' Peter replied. 'I have never eaten anything impure or unclean.' The voice spoke to him a second time, 'Do not call anything impure that God has made clean'"* (Acts 10:9-15, NIV). The vision had a literal meaning, as well as an allegorical sense to Peter -- Gentile believers in Christ were no longer unclean and could from that time on be baptized into the faith.

Paul preached, *"Eat anything sold in the meat market without raising questions of conscience, for, 'The earth is the Lord's, and everything in it.'"* (1 Cor 10:25-26, NIV). On another occasion he said, *"For every creature of God is good, and nothing to be refused, if it be received with thanksgiving: For it is sanctified by the word of God and prayer"* (1 Tim 4:4-5).

Men's hair and beard.
God commanded the men of Israel, *"Do not cut the hair at the sides of your head or clip off the edges of your beard"* (Lev 19:27, NIV). The sides of the head, aside from the cheeks,

include the temples. The mustache may be trimmed, as implied in 2 Samuel 19:24a (NKJV) -- *"Now Mephibosheth the son of Saul came down to meet the king. And he had not cared for his feet, nor trimmed his mustache…"*

Samson and Absalom were admired for their full hair (Judg 16:13-14,19; 2 Sam 14:25-26). The Shulamite sang of the locks of her beloved which were "bushy" (Song 5:11). Josephus wrote that Solomon's guards were distinguished by "luxuriant heads of hair" (Ant, VIII, vii, 3 [185]).[28] In Biblical times, the only men without beards were the eunuchs, castrated male servants in the households of royalty and nobility.[29] Baldness was considered embarrassing (2 Kings 2:23-24; Isa 3:24).[30]

In New Testament times, the Jews began adopting the Greek and Roman fashion of cutting the hair short (1 Cor 11:14-15),[31] but not as close as in our modern era, as we can see in religious paintings portraying Christ and the disciples.

Tattoos and skin cuttings.

God forbids His people from cutting their bodies or printing marks on their skin. *"You shall not make any cuttings in your flesh for the dead, nor tattoo any marks on you: I am the LORD"* (Lev 19:28, NKJV). Cutting and tattooing the body were part of the ceremonies and rituals by which pagans in the ancient world expressed their grief over the death of their loved ones.[32]

Any deliberate disfigurement of the human body is a desecration of the workmanship of God, after whose likeness man has been created.[33]

Sexual cleanness.

The Mosaic law for Israel has instructions for practically every aspect of life, including matters pertaining to relationships between sexually mature men and women.

Semen. A man's discharge produces uncleanness. *"When a man has an emission of semen, he must bathe his whole body with water, and he will be unclean till evening. Any clothing or leather that has semen on it must be washed with water, and it will be unclean till evening. When a man lies with a woman and there is an emission of semen, both must bathe with water, and they will be unclean till evening"* (Lev 15:16-18, NIV).

Menstruation. A woman's monthly period is particularly unclean. *"When a woman has her regular flow of blood, the impurity of her monthly period will last seven days, and anyone who touches her will be unclean till evening. Anything she lies on during her period will be unclean, and anything she sits on will be unclean. Whoever touches her bed must wash his clothes and bathe with water, and he will be unclean till evening"* (Lev 15:19-22, NIV).

Order and harmony.
God's prohibition on odd combinations may be puzzling to some. *"Do not mate different kinds of animals. Do not plant your field with two kinds of seed"* (Lev 19:19, NIV). *"Do not wear clothes of wool and linen woven together"* (Deut 22:11, NIV). These do not seem to be morally evil, but at times are even scientific, fashionable, or profitable, so many people today violate these injunctions, which are optional for them anyway.

But the reason Paul gave nearly 2,000 years ago is still valid. *"For God is not the author of confusion, but of peace..."* (1 Cor 14:33a). The bottom line apparently is order and harmony.

Seven feasts and holy days.
God appointed seven holy days for Israel: 1) Passover; 2) Feast of Unleavened Bread; 3) Firstfruits Wave offering; 4) Feast of Weeks (Feast of Harvest or Pentecost); 5) Feast of Trumpets; 6) Day of Atonement; and 7) Feast of Tabernacles (Feast of Booths, or Ingathering), (Lev. 23:4-44).

Passover. Observed on the 14th day of the first month in spring, Passover refers to the sacrifice of a lamb for each Hebrew family in Egypt, where the Israelites were slaves. They smeared the blood of the lamb on their doorposts as a sign to God's angel that he should "pass over" their houses when he destroyed all the firstborn of Egypt to persuade Pharaoh to let Israel go.

It was after midnight of this day that the Israelites left Egypt in the Exodus led by Moses.

Feast of Unleavened Bread. Beginning on the 15th day of the first month, this seven-day feast commemorates Israel's hasty departure from Egypt. Jews eat unleavened bread for seven days to show that the Israelites had no time to leaven the bread for their last meal in Egypt. Today, all products with yeast, baking powder or soda are removed from homes. *"Seven days shall there be no leaven found in your houses"* (Ex 12:19a).

Work on the first and seventh days is forbidden. *"On the first day hold a sacred assembly and do no regular work... And on the seventh day hold a sacred assembly and do no regular work"* (Lev 23:7,8b, NIV).

Feast of Firstfruits. This was made on the first day after the Sabbath during the Feast of Unleavened Bread, *"Speak unto the children of Israel, and say unto them, When ye be come into the land which I give unto you, and shall reap the harvest thereof, then ye shall bring a sheaf of the firstfruits of your harvest unto the priest: And he shall wave the sheaf before the LORD, to be accepted for you: on the morrow after the sabbath the priest shall wave it"* (Lev 23:10-11).

Pentecost (Feast of Weeks or Harvest). Celebrated annually, Pentecost ("fiftieth" in Greek), falls on the 50th day after the firstfruits wave offering (Lev 23:15-16, NIV).

A new firstfruits wave offering and two loaves of bread marked the beginning and end of the grain harvest.[34] Jews *"proclaim a sacred assembly and do no regular work"* (v. 21b).

Feast of Trumpets. *"On the first day of the seventh month hold a sacred assembly and do no regular work. It is a day for you to sound the trumpets"* (Num 29:2, NIV).

The Feast of Trumpets signals the beginning of the civil year in autumn. (Israel observed two new years. The first month in spring marked the start of the religious calendar -- Ex 12:2-ff.)

Day of Atonement. A high sabbath, *"The tenth day of this seventh month is the Day of Atonement. Hold a sacred assembly and deny yourselves, and present an offering made to the LORD by fire. Do no work on that day..."* (Lev 23:27-28a, NIV).

The most solemn holiday in Israel, this is a day of public fasting and humiliation as the nation of Israel seeks atonement for its sins (Lev 23:27; 16:29; Num 29:7). All the people are to "afflict their souls," that is, to fast (from the evening of the 9th to the evening of the 10th) under pain of getting cut off from Israel (Lev 23:27-32).

Feast of Tabernacles (Booths or Ingathering). During this feast, kept on the 15th-22nd days of the seventh month, Israel was to live in booths (temporary shelters of branches and twigs) in memory of their wilderness wandering. *"Say to the Israelites: `On the fifteenth day of the seventh month the LORD's Feast of Tabernacles begins, and it lasts for seven days. The first day is a sacred assembly; do no regular work ... on the eighth day hold a sacred assembly and present an offering made to the LORD by fire. It is the closing assembly; do no regular work"* (Lev 23:34-35a,36b, NIV). It is also called the "Feast of Ingathering," because it is when all the fruits of the field are gathered in."[35]

Three yearly assemblies.

Three festivals are annual holy days of pilgrimage. *"Three times in the year all thy males shall appear before the Lord GOD."* (Ex 23:17). These are the feasts of Unleavened Bread, Pentecost, and Tabernacles (Ex 23:14-16). Male Israelites from far and wide assembled at the Temple in Jerusalem or in one of the 48 Levitical cities where priests from the tribe of Levi resided to serve the religious and spiritual needs of the other tribes.

Even without the Temple, Jews and Messianic Gentiles today continue to observe the feasts appointed by God.

"Civil law" overview

The fourth division of the law consists of the God-given commandments for the theocratic governance of Israel. We read in *Nelson's Illustrated Bible Dictionary*, "What is often called the civil law includes those specific laws in the Pentateuch (first five books of the Old Testament) that regulate civil and social behavior. All such laws are fundamentally religious since God is the lawgiver and ruler over everything.

"There are eight distinct categories of civil law in the Old Testament: (1) laws regulating leaders, (2) laws regulating the army, (3) criminal laws, (4) laws dealing with crimes against property, (5) laws relating to humane treatment, (6) laws about personal and family rights, (7) laws about property rights, and (8) laws regulating other social behavior."[36]

"Eye for an eye." This phrase in the Mosaic Law (Ex 21:24) was not a harsh principle authorizing cruel punishment. Rather, it was the assurance of equality before the law. Each criminal had to justly pay for his crime (Num 35:31), unlike in some pagan nations, where the rich could buy their acquittal. Victims, on the other hand, could not inflict more injury than they had received. The law protected orphans, widows, slaves, and strangers from injustice (Ex 21:2,20-21; 22:21-23).[37]

Biblical law was more humane. Unlike those of other nations in the ancient world, it viewed human life as especially valuable. It avoided mutilations and other savage punishments. In Greece, the Spartans butchered their slaves. In Rome, where a master was murdered all the slaves within hearing were killed. They were punished over the littlest things. In Israel, the slave's life was guarded as carefully as the master's. If the master caused even the loss of a tooth, the slave was to be set free. The chastity of female slaves was strictly protected.[38]

Money and property. In Rome the creditor could imprison the debtor and even kill him according to law. In Israel, no crime against property incurred death -- restitution and fine were the usual penalty. Bond service until the sabbatical year was the extreme punishment. Thus, no Jew could be kept a slave for more than seven years, and after that he was to be sent away with generous gifts (Ex 21:7-26; Deut 15:13-15).[39]

Sexual offenses. Adulterers and engaged women who had relations with other men before marriage were stoned to death (Deut 22:13-22). Punishment for rape varied according to the circumstances. *"If a man happens to meet in a town a virgin pledged to be married and he sleeps with her, you shall take both of them to the gate of that town and stone them to death-- the girl because she was in a town and did not scream for help, and the man because he violated another man's wife... But if out in the country a man happens to meet a girl pledged to be married and rapes her, only the man who has done this shall die. Do nothing to the girl; she has committed no sin deserving death. This case is like that of someone who attacks and murders his neighbor, for the man found the girl out in the country, and though the betrothed girl screamed, there was no one to rescue her. If a man happens to meet a virgin who is not pledged to be married and rapes her and they are discovered, he shall pay the girl's father fifty shekels of silver. He must marry the girl, for he has violated her. He can never divorce her as long as he lives"* (Deut 22:23-29, NIV).

"Ceremonial law" overview

This fifth division of the 613 commandments consists of the rules and regulations for the priesthood and offerings to God. Called ceremonial law, its outline is in Exodus ch. 25-31.[40]

The priesthood. Priests officiated at worship by offering various offerings on behalf of the people and leading them in the confession of their sins. They acted as mediators between sinful man and God, offering sacrifices so that sin might be forgiven (Lev 4:20,26,31). Persons with physical defects or disqualifying diseases were not qualified to serve as priests (Lev 21:16-21). Physical perfection symbolized the priests' spiritual wholeness and holiness.

Their clothing carried great significance – the white linen garments stood for holiness and glory; coats woven in one piece without a seam indicated their spiritual integrity, wholeness, and righteousness. Ministering before God at the altar, the priests made sure the offerings of the people were proper and the rituals were carried out correctly. Otherwise, the people could not be cleansed of their sins.[41]

Sacrificial offerings.

There were seven kinds of sacrificial offering: sin, guilt (trespass in KJV), burnt, peace, grain (meat in KJV), heave and wave, and the red heifer.

Sin offering. This was for the forgiveness of sin (Lev 4:20, 26,31,35; 5:10) and cleansing (ceremonial purgation) from the pollution of sin in general (12:8; 14:20; 16:19; etc.).

Guilt offering. Also called trespass offering, it was regarded as representing ransom for one specific offense (unlike the sin offering, which atoned for the person as a whole).

Burnt offering. This symbolized the full surrender to God of the individual or the congregation for renewal and sanctification, as well as consecration to a way of life pleasing to God.

Peace offering. It came in three kinds: thank offering (in times of prosperity and success), votive offering (vow in asking for a certain blessing from God), and freewill offering (gratitude for God's bounties and prayer for their continuance).

Grain and drink offerings. These recognized God as the source of all earthly blessings by dedicating to Him the best of

His gifts -- flour, the main support of life; oil, symbol of richness; and wine, symbol of vigor and refreshment (Ps 104:15).

Heave and wave offerings. These were contributions for religious purposes (Isa 40:20), such as the maintenance of the sanctuary (Ex 25:2,8; 30:13; 35:5,21,24; 36:3,6; Ezra 8:25; etc.) or for the support of the priests.

Red heifer. A red heifer without blemish was burned with cedar wood, hyssop, and scarlet material. The ashes were used with running water to purify persons and things made unclean by contact with a dead body (Num 19:1-5).[42]

Tithing.

This is the practice of giving back a tenth of one's increase to God. The first Biblical instance is in Gen 14:17-20. Abraham, after rescuing Lot from his enemies, gave Melchizedek, "king of Salem" and "priest of God Most High," a tithe of all the goods he had won in battle. His grandson Jacob also promised to give to the Lord a tenth of all that he would ever gain (Gen 28:22). To tithe is to acknowledge God's ownership of everything on earth.

Told to Israel. The commandment was specifically told to Israel. *"And all the tithe of the land, whether of the seed of the land, or of the fruit of the tree, is the LORD's: it is holy unto the LORD"* (Lev 27:30-32). Its neglect amounted to sin. *"Will a man rob God? Yet ye have robbed me. But ye say, Wherein have we robbed thee? In tithes and offerings. Ye are cursed with a curse: for ye have robbed me, even this whole nation"* (Mal 3:8-9).

Overflowing blessings. On the other hand, its observance produces overflowing blessings. *"Bring ye all the tithes into the storehouse, that there may be meat in mine house, and prove me now herewith, saith the LORD of hosts, if I will not open you the windows of heaven, and pour you out a blessing, that there shall not be room enough to receive it"* (Mal 3:8-10).

For priests and Levites. The Mosaic law commanded that tithe should be paid to the Levites, who in turn must give a tenth of it to the priest (Num 18). But, after the return from Babylonian exile, the Levites had become very few compared to the priests (Ezra 2:36-42; 8:15-20,24-30; Neh 11:10-19). Josephus wrote that, later, tithes were paid to the priests, no longer to the Levites (Josephus, Ant, XX, viii, 8; ix, 2).[43]

Fat for the LORD only. The Israelites were forbidden to eat fat. *"Speak unto the children of Israel, saying, Ye shall eat no manner of fat, of ox, or of sheep, or of goat"* (Lev 7:23). As the richest and best part of the animal's flesh, the fat rightfully belongs only to God. Besides, it was the fat that fueled the fire of burnt sacrifices.

An exception seems to be implied. *"Anyone who eats the fat of an animal from which an offering by fire may be made to the LORD must be cut off from his people"* (Lev 7:25, NIV). Does this verse suggest that, if an animal was slaughtered not for sacrifice but solely for food, the fat could be eaten?

Deuteronomy 12:15a appears to allow the consumption of fat: *"However, you may slaughter and eat meat within all your gates, whatever your heart desires..."* (NKJV).

Life... or death?

The choice is ours. *"See, I have set before you today life and prosperity, and death and adversity... I call heaven and earth to witness against you today, that I have set before you life and death, the blessing and the curse. So choose life in order that you may live, you and your descendants"* (Deut 30:15,19, NASU).

Prophecy says many will pass up this offer. *"For the time will come when men will not put up with sound doctrine. Instead, to suit their own desires, they will gather around them a great number of teachers to say what their itching ears want to hear"* (2 Tim 4:3-4, NIV). So, will you be like those who listen only to what they want to hear? Or will you listen to what God wants you to do?

Will you keep both "great" and "least" commandments, or just the "great," mandatory ones? Will you be called "great" or "least" in the kingdom of heaven? Will you be in the first resurrection at the Second Coming of Christ, or in the second resurrection 1,000 years later for the Last Judgment? Will you be part of the 144,000 elect, or one of the 100 million saints, or, heavens!, neither of the two?

7

Secrets of the Soul and Spirit

I pray God your whole spirit and soul and body be preserved blameless unto the coming of our Lord Jesus Christ.

--1 Thessalonians 5:23a

What happens when a person dies? What is the soul? And what is the spirit? Are they two different things? Or are they one and the same? Most people think they are the same, as the two words are often used synonymously, without distinction. *The New Unger's Bible Dictionary* says that it is not unusual: "The two terms are often used interchangeably, the same functions being ascribed to each... Theologians have pored over these distinctions ceaselessly."[1]

Soul and spirit

The Bible itself, however, sheds light on the matter. *"For the word of God is quick, and powerful, and sharper than any twoedged sword, piercing even to the dividing asunder of soul and spirit, and of the joints and marrow, and is a discerner of the thoughts and intents of the heart"* (Heb 4:12).

Paul says the soul and the spirit can be separated; so it becomes certain that the soul and the spirit are two different things. Adding credence to this is the fact that they have different names in the original languages of the Bible. "Soul" is from the Hebrew *nephesh* and Greek *psuche* (*psyche*), while "spirit" is translated from the Hebrew *ruach* and Greek *pneuma.*

Paul also contrasted the soul against the spirit in his first letter to the Corinthians: *"And so it is written, The first man Adam was made a living soul (psuche); the last Adam was made a quickening spirit (pneuma)"* (v. 15:45).

The parts of a man

In 1 Thessalonians 5:23, Paul enumerated three parts of a man: *"And the very God of peace sanctify you wholly; and I pray God your whole spirit and soul and body be preserved blameless unto the coming of our Lord Jesus Christ."* The three named parts are, to repeat: (1) the spirit; (2) the soul; and (3) the body. Let us examine each one.

The Body.

There is no exact term for "body" in the Hebrew tongue. The *International Standard Bible Encyclopaedia* explains: "Generally speaking, the Old Testament language employs no fixed term for the human body as an entire organism. Various terms were employed, each of which denotes only one part or element of the physical nature, such as 'trunk,' 'bones,' 'belly,' 'bowels,' 'reins,' 'flesh,' these parts being used, by synecdoche, for the whole... The Greek word which is used almost exclusively for 'body' in the New Testament is soma,"[2]

Man's physical body came from the earth. *"And the LORD God formed man of the dust of the ground..."* (Gen 2:7a). Chemically, human beings are made up of the same elements found in the ground.

As it is, the body is the physical container of the ethereal or spiritual parts of man. To use a computer age analogy, the body is hardware, while the soul and the spirit are software that makes it work. Like software, the soul and spirit have no mass.

The soul.

In Genesis 2:7 -- *"And the LORD God formed man of the dust of the ground, and breathed into his nostrils the breath of life; and man became a living soul."* From this verse, it looks like the soul comes into existence as a product or result of life.

The idea is supported by the Biblical information that both man and animals have souls. The phrase *"living soul"* in Genesis 2:7b is *"nepesh chayah"* in Hebrew. In the line *"God said, Let the earth bring forth the living creature after his kind, cattle, and creeping thing, and beast of the earth after his kind"* (Gen 1:24b), *"living creature"* is also *"nepesh chayah."*

Instincts. The soul feels and expresses some of the most basic instincts and emotions of man. According to *Fausset's Bible Dictionary*, "The soul is the seat of the appetites, the desires, the will; hunger, thirst, sorrow, joy; love, hope, fear, etc…"[3] It is the soul that feels hunger and thirst, as in Isaiah 29:8 (NKJV) – *"It shall even be as when a hungry man dreams. And look -- he eats; But he awakes, and his soul is still empty; Or as when a thirsty man dreams, And look -- he drinks; But he awakes, and indeed he is faint, And his soul still craves."* Deuteronomy 12:20 – *"When the LORD thy God shall enlarge thy border, as he hath promised thee, and thou shalt say, I will eat flesh, because thy soul longeth to eat flesh; thou mayest eat flesh, whatsoever thy soul lusteth after."* Psalm 107:9 -- *"For he satisfieth the longing soul, and filleth the hungry soul with goodness."* Proverb 25:25 – *"As cold waters to a thirsty soul, so is good news from a far country."*

Carl Jung (1875-1961), renowned Swiss psychiatrist who developed the field of analytical psychology, wholly concurs: The soul or *nephesh* is the lower nature of man, the personal unconscious with the instincts and desires.[4]

Strong emotions. It is also the soul that experiences and manifests the wide spectrum of human emotions – such as joy, *"Rejoice the soul of thy servant: for unto thee, O Lord, do I lift up my soul"* (Ps 86:4); sorrow, *"Then saith he unto them, My soul is exceeding sorrowful, even unto death: tarry ye here, and watch with me"* (Matt 26:38); love, *"Tell me, O thou whom my soul loveth…"* (Song 1:7a); hate, *"And I will set my tabernacle among you: and my soul shall not abhor you"* (Lev 26:11); fear, *"And fear came upon every soul…"* (Acts 2:43a).

A person or a creature. *Fausset's Bible Dictionary* says that "soul" is also used to refer to the man himself, a person, the self, a creature,[5] as in 1 Peter 3:20b -- *"...the longsuffering of God waited in the days of Noah, while the ark was a preparing, wherein few, that is, eight souls were saved by water"*; 1 Sam 20:17 -- *"And Jonathan caused David to swear again, because he loved him: for he loved him as he loved his own soul"*; Ps 74:19 -- *"O deliver not the soul of thy turtledove unto the multitude of the wicked..."*

The spirit.

Strangely, the Jews had disparate views on the spirit. *"For the Sadducees say that there is no resurrection, neither angel, nor spirit: but the Pharisees confess both* (Acts 23:8). It seems that the Sadducees were wrong, and the Pharisees were right.

The *International Standard Bible Encyclopaedia* states that the term "spirit" has a shade of meaning that is "generally for all the manifestations of the spiritual part in man, as that which thinks, feels, wills..."[6]

Mind. In short, the spirit (*ruach*) houses the intellect, the mental faculties, or the rational, thinking mind of man.

Roberto Assagioli, an Italian Jew regarded as the father of transpersonal psychology, defined the *ruach* ("spirit") as the personal "I" or "conscious self."[7]

Many times in the OT, *ruach* ("spirit") is translated "mind": (Gen 26:34-35) *"And Esau was forty years old when he took to wife Judith the daughter of Beeri the Hittite, and Bashemath the daughter of Elon the Hittite: Which were a grief of mind (ruach) unto Isaac and to Rebekah"*; (Prov 29:11) *"A fool uttereth all his mind (ruach): but a wise man keepeth it in till afterwards"*; (Ezek 11:5b) *"Thus have ye said, O house of Israel: for I know the things that come into your mind (ruach), every one of them"*; (Dan 5:20a) *"But when his heart was lifted up, and his mind (ruach) hardened in pride..."*; (Hab 1:11) *"Then shall his mind (ruach) change, and he shall pass over, and offend, imputing this his power unto his god."* As such, the spirit (*ruach*) can:

Have knowledge, wisdom. *"And thou shalt speak unto all that are wise hearted, whom I have filled with the spirit (ruach) of wisdom..."* (Ex 28:3a); *"Inasmuch as an excellent spirit (ruach), knowledge, understanding, interpreting dreams, solving riddles, and explaining enigmas were found in this Daniel..."*

(Dan 5:12a, NKJV). The usage persisted till the time of Christ: *"Immediately Jesus knew in his spirit (pneuma) that this was what they were thinking in their hearts, and he said to them, "Why are you thinking these things?"* (Mark 2:8-9, NIV).

Make decisions. *"But Sihon king of Heshbon would not let us pass by him: for the LORD thy God hardened his spirit (ruach), and made his heart obstinate..."* (Deut 2:30a); *"Watch and pray so that you will not fall into temptation. The spirit (pneuma) is willing, but the body is weak"* (Matt 26:41, NIV).

Be upset. *"And it came to pass in the morning that his spirit was troubled..."* (Gen 41:8a); *"Now in the second year of the reign of Nebuchadnezzar, Nebuchadnezzar had dreams; and his spirit was troubled and his sleep left him"* (Dan 2:1, NASU).

Be patient or proud. *"Better is the end of a thing than the beginning thereof: and the patient in spirit is better than the proud in spirit (ruach)"* (Eccl 7:8). Thus, the spirit can have all the thoughts that may enter into a man's mind.

God and His angels

God is a spirit (John 4:24). And, as we know, God is the all-knowing Intelligence or Mind outside space-time.

The angels, too, are spirits (Ps 104:4, Heb 1:7,12:9). And the angels, unless they materialize, have neither physical bodies nor souls. Yet, although ethereal, they have individual consciousness and minds of their own. This goes to show that the mind, consciousness, and intelligence are in the spirit.

Spirits of animals.

Animals have spirits (*ruach*), too. The Bible tells us: *"Who knoweth the spirit of man that goeth upward, and the spirit of the beast that goeth downward to the earth?"* (Eccl 3:21).

At death, perhaps due to their very limited mental abilities and absence of reasoning power, the spirits of animals return to the ground. Besides, animals are not morally responsible creatures and so cannot sin, unlike men.

The parts of Adam.

Did Adam have all three parts when he was created? Let us reread the verse on his creation. *"And the LORD God formed* man of the dust of the ground, and breathed into his nostrils the breath of life; and man became a living soul"* (Gen 2:7). (In this verse, the Hebrew word used for "breath" is *neshamah*.)

No spirit.

Something seems to be missing. Adam had a physical body from the dust of the ground, and as a result of life he became a living soul (*nephesh*), having the instincts necessary to eat and drink to sustain life; but... he had no spirit (*ruach*)! Adam lacked the element that we have just seen is supposed to be responsible for self-consciousness and intelligent thought! What could be the reason for this?

The prophet Zechariah gives us an idea: "*The burden of the word of the LORD for Israel, saith the LORD, which stretcheth forth the heavens, and layeth the foundation of the earth, and formeth the spirit of man within him"* (Zech 12:1). God forms the spirit inside man. Hence, it follows that, the physical body must first come into existence; and only then can the spirit (*ruach*) be divinely fashioned inside the human body.

The process becomes clearer. First, the body; next the soul (*nephesh*, with the instincts to survive by drinking, eating, etc.) appears as a result of life in the body; then the spirit (ruach, with its consciousness and intellect) is formed and gradually develops, just as the physical body grows and matures, presumably at the same rate – much like that of a newborn child.

Psychoanalyst Carl Jung taught the same thing: the conscious mind "grows out of an unconscious psyche, which is older than it..."[8] This explains why we cannot talk sensibly with babies and very young children – their *ruach* (spirit or mind) is not yet well developed. If that is the case, then God had created Adam as an infant or a little baby!

A fourth part of man

Man appears to have a little known fourth part, in addition to the three we have already discussed.

Two kinds of spirit.

Another kind of spirit distinct from the *ruach* crops up surreptitiously, unnoticeably, in some Biblical verses. And so we see two markedly different kinds of spirit: One seems to be perishable, while the other is indestructible.

We have read in 1 Thessalonians 5:23: *"And the very God of peace sanctify you wholly; and I pray God your whole spirit and soul and body be preserved blameless unto the coming of our Lord Jesus Christ."* Since Paul prayed for the preservation of the spirit; we take it that the spirit can be destroyed.

We see the same thing in other verses, both in the OT and NT: *"Thou hast granted me life and favour, and thy visitation hath preserved my spirit"* (Job 10:12); *"To deliver such an one unto Satan for the destruction of the flesh, that the spirit may be saved in the day of the Lord Jesus"* (1 Cor 5:5).

On the other hand, there seems to be another kind of spirit that cannot be destroyed. *"Then shall the dust return to the earth as it was: and the spirit shall return unto God who gave it"* (Eccl 12:7). Solomon declared that the spirit of the dead will return to God, who has given it to man. But, as we have learned from Zechariah 12:1, the spirit (*ruach,* "mind") is formed internally in the body – it did not come from God.

So, herein lies the difference. The perishable spirit does not come from God and, if soiled by sin, can be destroyed in hell; whereas the indestructible spirit has been given by God and, at death, will return to God unconditionally -- whether the person is a sinner or a saint. These are definitely two kinds of spirit.

We are already familiar with the first kind of spirit. Let us look for examples of the second one for a closer examination.

"Spirit of life." Several passages tell of a spirit that makes the body alive. *"It is the Spirit who gives life; the flesh profits nothing. The words that I speak to you are spirit, and they are life"* (John 6:63-64, NKJV); *"For as the body without the spirit is dead, so faith without works is dead also"* (James 2:26); *"And all wept, and bewailed her: but he said, Weep not; she is not dead, but sleepeth. And they laughed him to scorn, knowing that she was dead. And he put them all out, and took her by the hand, and called, saying, Maid, arise. And her spirit came again, and she arose straightway: and he commanded to give her meat"* (Luke 8:52-55); *"And after three days and an half the Spirit of life from God entered into them, and they stood upon their feet; and great fear fell upon them which saw them"* (Rev 11:11).

"Breath of life." In other Bible verses, the life-sustaining element in man is called "breath of life." *"The Spirit of God hath made me, and the breath (neshamah) of the Almighty hath given me life"* (Job 33:4); *"Thus saith God the LORD, he that created the heavens, and stretched them out; he that spread forth the earth, and that which cometh out of it; he that giveth breath (neshamah) unto the people upon it, and spirit (ruach) to them that walk therein* (Isa 42:5).

The *ruach* and the *neshamah* are mentioned together as if the same in Job 34:14-15: *"If he set his heart upon man, if he gather unto himself his spirit (ruach) and his breath (neshamah); All flesh shall perish together, and man shall turn again unto dust"* (Job 34:14-15).

The breath of life in man came from God. Hence, the spirit of life referred to must be the indestructible *neshamah*, which *"shall return unto God who gave it,"* whether the person is righteous or sinful. The other spirit with the mind (*ruach*) that grows with the body is thus corruptible and can either be saved or destroyed.

Both animals and man are called "*living creatures*" in the Bible (Gen 9:10-16), translated from *nephesh chayah* in Hebrew. Yet, what puts man above animals is the Biblical fact that, with the first man, God "*breathed into his nostrils the breath of life*" – the divine *neshamah*.

The Jewish teaching.

The writings of the Jewish sages enlighten us further. "The *nephesh* possesses in itself no light and cannot out of its own being engender it, and for this reason it is in close connection and deeply enmeshed with its body. The *ruah* rides upon the *nephesh*, dominates it, and enlightens it with supernal glory, as much as it can bear; this *nephesh* is the throne of the *ruah*. The *neshamah* produces the *ruah*, rules over it, and sheds upon it the light of life. The *ruah* depends entirely upon the *neshamah* and it is lit up by its light and nourished by its celestial food, while the *nephesh* is similarly dependent on the *ruah*."[9]

We can now visualize a more complete picture based on the Scriptural accounts and Jewish writings: First, God formed the body of Adam from the earth; next, the body was made alive by the *neshamah* (breath) from God; the *nephesh* (soul) then came about spontaneously as a result of life; and then, lastly, the *neshamah* produced the *ruach* (mind), although more slowly. The *neshamah* then lighted up the *ruach,* and the *ruach* in turn lighted up the *nephesh.*

The four parts of man.
In summary, the four parts that make up a man are:
1. The "body" that came from the "dust of the ground";
2. The *neshamah* or "breath of life" (also called "spirit of life") from God that gives life to the body;
3, The *nephesh* or "soul" that comes with life, with the instincts to sustain and preserve life, as well as reproduce; and
4. The ruach or "spirit" that forms inside the body and has the consciousness, intellect, and mind of man.

Descendants of Adam

If that was how the four parts of the first man, Adam, came together, is the process still the same with us, his descendants? Obviously, God no longer forms the body of man from the dust, it comes from the parents. But what about the three ethereal parts (*neshamah, nephesh,* and *ruach*), does God still breathe into the nostrils of each and every newborn child?

The New Unger's Bible Dictionary informs us: "The origin of man's immaterial nature is subject to three theories: (1) The creational, maintaining that soul and spirit are created at birth. (2) Traducian. Soul and spirit are generated the same as the body. (3) The soul is preexistent, embracing the idea of transmigration of souls."[10] Let us examine these three theories under the magnifying glass of reason one by one.

Preexistence theory.
Belief in the preexistence of the soul before its union with the body is closely linked to reincarnation – rebirth of the soul in a new human body, in an animal, or in some other form of life. This was an idea that came with the Greek culture to Judea and became known to the Jews, finding its way to the Bible. *"And his disciples asked him, saying, Master, who did sin, this man, or his parents, that he was born blind?"* (John 9:2). The disciples

were wondering if the beggar might have been born blind because he had sinned in a previous life.

Christ said no, the man was born blind so that the works of God could be seen through him. Moreover, Paul, in a sweeping statement later, doused any notion that disciples might have entertained about reincarnation. *"And as it is appointed unto men once to die, but after this the judgment"* (Heb 9:27). He categorically declared that men can only die once. The preexistence theory, therefore, is unbiblical.

Creation theory.

Wikipedia, the internet encyclopedia, states that, "The early Church Fathers universally agreed that the soul of Adam was directly created by God." Later on, "some of the later Fathers — most notably Saint Augustine…— began to question the creation by God of individual souls and to incline to the opposite opinion (Traducianism), which seemed to facilitate the explanation of the transmission of original sin…"[11]

Furthermore, God's creation is supposed to have been finished after the first six days (Gen 2:2), so that no new souls, if ever, are being created directly any more.

Traducian theory.

The same source tells us: "Traducianism means that this immaterial aspect is transmitted through natural generation along with the body, the material aspect of man. That is, an individual's soul is derived from the souls of the individual's parents. This implies that only the soul of Adam was created directly by God (with Eve's substance, material and immaterial, being taken from out of Adam)…"[12]

The term "Traducian" is descriptive, coming from the Latin word *traducere*, which, among other things, means "to lead across, transfer."

Traducianists point out that, after Adam sinned, all men are sinful from conception (Ps 51:5 – "*I was shapen in iniquity; and in sin did my mother conceive me*") to birth (Job 14:4 – "*Who can bring a clean thing out of an unclean?*"; cf. Ps 15:14 and 58:3). God will not create anything sinful, so it follows that new souls are not created, they are passed down.

Further proof is the Biblical implication that the souls of offspring are already present in their parents long before they are born (Gen 46:26 -- *"All the souls that came with Jacob into Egypt, which came out of his loins..."*; Heb 7:9-10 -- *"Levi also, who receiveth tithes, payed tithes in Abraham. For he was yet in the loins of his father, when Melchisedec met him."*).

Separated at death

King Solomon says there is an invisible silver cord or string, figurative or literal, that keeps the body and the soul and the spirit tied together, but this gets unfastened at the moment of death. We read in Ecclesiastes 12:6-7 – *"Or ever the silver cord be loosed, or the golden bowl be broken, or the pitcher be broken at the fountain, or the wheel broken at the cistern. Then shall the dust return to the earth as it was: and the spirit shall return unto God who gave it."*

Matthew Henry's Commentary explains the passage quite literally: "Then shall the silver cord, by which soul and body were wonderfully fastened together, be loosed, that sacred knot untied, and those old friends be forced to part..."[13]

Death can no longer be averted once the silver cord is loosed. *"There is no man that hath power over the spirit to retain the spirit; neither hath he power in the day of death: and there is no discharge in that war; neither shall wickedness deliver those that are given to it"* (Eccl 8:8).

That brings us to an ages-old question: What happens to the soul and spirit when a person dies? The enigma of whether life continues after death must have haunted men since Adam died.

"Sleep of death"?

Many times in the Scriptures, death is euphemistically called "sleep." For this reason, some denominations teach that dead people will lie in the grave with no consciousness whatsoever until they are raised back to life in the two resurrections.

The teaching is based on a number of Biblical verses, such as 1 Kings 2:10 -- *"So David slept with his fathers, and was buried in the city of David"*; Matthew 27:52a -- *"And the graves were opened; and many bodies of the saints which slept arose..."*; 1 Corinthians 15:20,51 -- *"But now is Christ risen from the dead, and become the firstfruits of them that slept";* *"Behold, I shew you a mystery; We shall not all sleep, but we shall all be changed;* Ecclesiastes 9:5 -- *"For the living know that they shall die: but the dead know not any thing, neither have they any more a reward; for the memory of them is forgotten."*

Conscious spirits. Revelation 6:9-10, however, belies that teaching. *"And when he had opened the fifth seal, I saw under the altar the souls of them that were slain for the word of God, and for the testimony which they held: And they cried with a loud voice, saying, How long, O Lord, holy and true, dost thou not judge and avenge our blood on them that dwell on the earth?"* The martyred believers are fully conscious and calling to God from below the altar!

Moreover, Christ had said to the dying thief crucified with Him, *"Verily I say unto thee, To day shalt thou be with me in paradise"* (Luke 23:43b).

Heaven or hell?

After life in this world, do people who have done good go to heaven, while those who were bad are thrown into hell?

All children go to heaven?

It is commonly believed that the spirits of innocent young children who die go straight to heaven. Can this be true?

As we have seen in Psalm 51:5, every child is *"shapen in iniquity; and in sin did my mother conceive me."* Everyone therefore is a sinner even while still in the womb! That is because we have inherited a sinful nature from our ancestor, Adam. *"For as by one man's disobedience many were made sinners..."* (Rom 5:19a). Paul adds that we are naturally the object of divine anger. *"Among whom also we all had our conversation in times past in the lusts of our flesh, fulfilling the desires of the flesh and of the mind; and were by nature the children of wrath, even as others"* (Eph 2:3). Sadly, not all dead children go to heaven.

No man in heaven. Christ had said, *"And no man hath ascended up to heaven, but he that came down from heaven, even the Son of man which is in heaven"* (John 3:13). Hence, no man who has been born on earth, except Christ, the Son of God, has ever gone up to be with the Almighty Father.

No one in hell… yet. The lake of fire has been made for the devil and his demons. *"Then shall he say also unto them on the left hand, Depart from me, ye cursed, into everlasting fire, prepared for the devil and his angels"* (Matt 25:41). As the Bible tells us, after the war in heaven Satan and his demons were cast down to earth, not into the lake of fire (Rev 12:9). In fact, Satan is now the reigning "god of this world" (2 Cor 4:4).

Jewish view of death

So, what really happens after death? Let us again appeal to the esoteric knowledge of the Jewish sages.

Three separate dwellings.

We read from a commentary on the Torah: "Three names has the soul of man: *nephesh, ruah* and *neshamah*. They are all comprised one within the other, yet upon death they have three distinct abodes:

"**Neshamah** ("breath of life") ascends at once to her place, the region from whence she emanated, and for her sake the light is kindled to shine above. She never again descends to earth… And as long as she has not ascended to be united with the Throne, the *ruah* (spirit) cannot crown itself in paradise, nor can the *nephesh* (soul) be at ease in its place; but when she ascends all the others find rest."[14]

This is in complete agreement with what Solomon wrote. *"Then shall the dust return to the earth as it was: and the spirit shall return unto God who gave it"* (Eccl 12:7).

"**Ruah** ("spirit") enters paradise and there dons a likeness which is in the semblance of the body: that likeness being, as it were, a garment with which the spirit robes itself, so that it may enjoy the delights of paradise."[15]

This is why Christ told the repentant thief crucified with Him, *"Verily I say unto thee, To day shalt thou be with me in paradise"* (Luke 23:43b).

Knowing the spirit of the dead will go to Paradise, the psalmist confidently sang, *"Into thine hand I commit my spirit: thou hast redeemed me, O LORD God of truth"* (Ps 31:5). Christ Himself commended to God His spirit, not his soul, as He was about to die on the cross: *"And when Jesus had cried out with a loud voice, He said, "Father, 'into Your hands I commit My spirit.' Having said this, He breathed His last"* (Luke 23:46-47, NKJV). The martyr Stephen likewise prayed for his spirit: *"And they stoned Stephen, calling upon God, and saying, Lord Jesus, receive my spirit"* (Acts 7:59).

"***Nephesh*** ("soul") remains in the grave until the body is decomposed and turned into dust, during which time it flits about in this world, seeking to mingle with the living... the three are one – yet separate. The *neshamah* ascends aloft to the fountain-head; the *ruah* enters paradise; the *nephesh* finds rest in the grave."[16]

Ghosts.

It appears that what is called "ghost" is the *nephesh*. Men have known and believed in ghosts since ancient times. Over 4,000 years ago, Job's friend Eliphaz described one in a verse we are now familiar with. *"Then a spirit passed before my face; the hair of my flesh stood up"* (Job 4:15).

The disciples mistook Christ for a ghost a few times. *"During the fourth watch of the night Jesus went out to them, walking on the lake. When the disciples saw him walking on the lake, they were terrified. "It's a ghost," they said, and cried out in fear"* (Matt 14:25-26, NIV). *"...but when they saw him walking on the lake, they thought he was a ghost"* (Mark 6:49, NIV).

After the Resurrection, *"While they were still talking about this, Jesus himself stood among them and said to them, 'Peace be with you.' They were startled and frightened, thinking they saw a ghost. He said to them, "Why are you troubled, and why do doubts rise in your minds? Look at my hands and my feet. It is I myself! Touch me and see; a ghost does not have flesh and bones, as you see I have"* (Luke 24:36-39, NIV).

Spiritism. According to the Jewish sages, the dead can be contacted. "Now when the children of men are in sorrow or trouble, and repair to the graves of the departed, then the *nephesh* is awakened and it wanders forth and rouses the *ruah*, which in turn rouses the Patriarchs, and then the *neshamah*."[17]

Thus we are told that, when invoked, all three – *nephesh*, *ruach*, and *neshamah* – reunite to appear before men. The witch of Endor summoned the spirit of the prophet Samuel: *"And the king said unto her, Be not afraid: for what sawest thou? And the woman said unto Saul, I saw gods ascending out of the earth. And he said unto her, What form is he of? And she said, An old man cometh up; and he is covered with a mantle. And Saul perceived that it was Samuel, and he stooped with his face to the ground, and bowed himself. And Samuel said to Saul, Why hast thou disquieted me, to bring me up?"* (1 Sam 28:13-15a).

Moses and Elijah appeared to Christ and the disciples at the Transfiguration on the mount. *"And, behold, there appeared unto them Moses and Elias talking with him"* (Matt 17:3).

Ordinarily, though, the *nephesh* of the dead seems to be a mere shadow that disintegrates sooner or later. It does not have a *ruach* (mind); that is why ghosts in general do not interact with people. It will only do so if the *nephesh* is rejoined by the *ruach* and the *neshamah*; or... if it is possessed by a spirit.

Wave frequency. From a quasi-scientific standpoint, some say that the endurance of the soul, being energy, depends a great deal on its wavelengths and frequencies, The higher the wave frequency, the stronger the energy.

When excited by strong emotions, the frequency of the waves increases, and the soul energy becomes stronger. That is why the souls of people who have died with intense emotions – such as anguish, bitterness, terror, etc. – are seen as "ghosts" for a much longer period of time than the souls of those who have died peacefully. For example, some "ghosts" seen dragging chains in castle dungeons are reported for hundreds of years.

Abomination to God. Summoning the spirits of dead people is disgusting to God. *"There shall not be found among you... a medium, or a spiritist, or one who calls up the dead. For all who do these things are an abomination to the LORD..."* (Deut 18:10a,11b-12a, NKJV).

The afterlife, according to Christ

The following account, related by Christ to His disciples, is not a parable, as some mistakenly believe, but an object lesson or practical example and illustration of what actually happens to the spirits of men after death.

"There was a certain rich man, which was clothed in purple and fine linen, and fared sumptuously every day: And there was

a certain beggar named Lazarus, which was laid at his gate, full of sores, And desiring to be fed with the crumbs which fell from the rich man's table: moreover the dogs came and licked his sores. And it came to pass, that the beggar died, and was carried by the angels into Abraham's bosom: the rich man also died, and was buried" (Luke 16:19-22).

The beggar is typical of the poor who will be God's heirs, as in Luke 6:20b (*"Blessed be ye poor: for yours is the kingdom of God."*); while the rich man is representative of the wealthy who will find it difficult to enter the kingdom of heaven, as in Mark 10:25 (*"It is easier for a camel to go through the eye of a needle, than for a rich man to enter into the kingdom of God."*)

As Christ lamented, *"For what will it profit a man if he gains the whole world, and loses his own soul?"* (Mark 8:36, NKJV).

Two regions in "hell"

Lazarus the beggar (personifying God's heirs, the saints) and the rich man went to two separate destinations after death. The rich man had a rude surprise. *"And in hell he lift up his eyes, being in torments, and seeth Abraham afar off, and Lazarus in his bosom"* (Luke 16:23). "Hell" here is the English translation of the Greek *Hades*, which refers to the underground region of the dead (not the lake of fire); its equivalent in Hebrew is *Sheol*.

The *International Standard Bible Encyclopaedia* comments: "Luke 16:23 is the only one which might seem to teach that recipients of salvation enter after death into Hades as a place of abode. It has been held that Hades is here the comprehensive designation of the locality where the dead reside, and is divided into two regions, 'the bosom of Abraham' and the place of torment, a representation for which Jewish parallels can be quoted, aside from its resemblance to the Greek bisection of Hades"[18]

Jewish historian Josephus wrote: "There is one descent into this region, at whose gate we believe there stands an archangel with an host, which gate when those pass through that are conducted down by the angels appointed over souls; they do not go the same way; but the just are guided to the right hand, and are led with hymns, sung by the angels appointed over that place unto a region of light, in which the just have dwelt from the beginning of the world; not constrained by necessity, but ever enjoying the prospect of the good things they see, and rejoice in the expectation of those new enjoyments, which will be peculiar to every one of them, and esteeming those things beyond what we have here; with whom there is no place of toil, no burning heat, no piercing cold, nor are any briers there; but the countenance of the fathers and of the just, which they see always smiles upon them, while they wait for that rest and eternal new life in heaven, which is to succeed this region. This place we call the Bosom of Abraham."[19]

The New Unger's Bible Dictionary thus concludes that "it seems clear that Hades was in two compartments, the residence respectively of saved and unsaved spirits."[20]

Region of the righteous.
According to *Matthew Henry's Commentary on the Whole Bible*, "The Jews expressed the happiness of the righteous at death three ways: they go to the garden of Eden: they go to be under the throne of glory; and they go to the bosom of Abraham..."[21] Says *The New Unger's Bible Dictionary*, 'Paradise' and 'Abraham's bosom,' both common Jewish terms of the day, were adopted by Christ in Luke 16:22 and 23:43 to designate the condition of the righteous in the intermediate state. The blessed dead, being with Abraham, were conscious and 'comforted' (16:25). The dying thief was on that very day to be with Christ in Paradise."[22]

Bosom of Abraham. It "is this which our Saviour here makes use of. Abraham was the father of the faithful; and whither should the souls of the faithful be gathered but to him, who, as a tender father, lays them in his bosom, especially at their first coming, to bid them welcome, and to refresh them when newly come from the sorrows and fatigue of this world?"[23]

Note that all of the saved, whether Jews or Gentiles, go to the "bosom of Abraham." After all, *"if ye be Christ's, then are ye Abraham's seed, and heirs according to the promise"* (Gal 3:29).

Under the throne. The phrase "under the throne of glory" means the same thing as "under the altar." In Exodus 30:1,6, God told Moses: *"And thou shalt make an altar to burn incense upon: of shittim wood shalt thou make it... And thou shalt put it* *before the vail that is by the ark of the testimony, before the mercy seat that is over the testimony, where I will meet with thee."* The altar of incense, symbolic of the altar in heaven, is before the mercy seat that stands for the throne of God.

The altar in heaven is also in front of God. *"And the sixth angel sounded, and I heard a voice from the four horns of the golden altar which is before God"* (Rev 6:13). Hence, the place "under the altar" is the selfsame place where righteous men go to after death. *"And when he had opened the fifth seal, I saw under the altar the souls of them that were slain for the word of God, and for the testimony which they held"* (Rev 6:9).

Gan Eden. The place of the saved was also known to the Jews as *Gan-Eden* ("Garden of Eden"), which, as most of us know, is synonymous to Paradise.

Third heaven. Paradise is also the "third heaven," as Paul illustrates in 2 Corinthians 12:2,4a – *"I knew a man in Christ above fourteen years ago, (whether in the body, I cannot tell; or whether out of the body, I cannot tell: God knoweth;) such an one caught up to the third heaven... How that he was caught up into paradise..."*

"Third heaven"? Jewish mystics taught that there were multiple heavens. *The Zondervan Pictorial Encyclopedia of the Bible* (vol. 1, p. 982) notes that the plural "heavens" includes "the place of God's residence." We find hints about this in the Scriptures. *"Behold, the heaven and the heaven of heavens is the LORD's thy God, the earth also, with all that therein is"* (Deut 10:14). "Later Judaism reckoned seven heavens."[24]

Seven heavens. The seven heavens have names and descriptions in Jewish mysticism: The first or lowest heaven is the so-called "*vilon*" or "curtain"; the second heaven is "*raqia*" or "firmament of heaven," the heaven of the sun, moon and stars; the third heaven is "*shahaqim*," where manna is ground for the pious; the fourth heaven is "*sebol*," the exalted Jerusalem and altar; the fifth heaven is "*maon*," the heaven of ministering angels; the sixth heaven is "*mahon*," the treasure chamber of the snow and rainbow; and the seventh heaven is "*aravot*," where dwell justice, righteousness, virtues, life and peace.[25] Although not found in Scriptures, these teachings are nevertheless favored by some scholars.

King Solomon's throne was symbolic of God's throne in the seventh heaven. There were six steps to his throne, representing six heavens. *"The throne had six steps..."* (1 Kings 10:19a, NIV). The golden footstool served as the seventh step – thus making seven levels in all, corresponding to the seven heavens.

Gehenna.
Let us now see the place where the rich man ended up after a lavish life on earth. *"And in hell he lift up his eyes, being in torments, and seeth Abraham afar off, and Lazarus in his bosom"* (Luke 16:23). Josephus gives us a detailed account: "But as to the unjust, they are dragged by force to the left hand by angels allotted for punishment, no longer going with a goodwill, but as prisoners driven by violence; to whom are sent the angels appointed over them to reproach them and threaten them with terrible looks, and to thrust them still downwards. Now those angels that are set over these souls, drag them into the neighborhood of hell itself, who, when they are hard by it, continually hear the noise of it, and do not stand clear of the hot vapor itself; but when they have a nearer view of this spectacle, as of a terrible and exceeding great prospect of fire, they are struck with a fearful expectation of a future judgment, and in effect punished thereby..."[26]

That terrifying region on the left is known as *Gehenna*, Greek for *Ge-Hinnom* ("Valley of Hinnom), an actual deep, narrow glen below the southern slope of Jerusalem. It had an area called Topeth, where pagan worshippers sacrificed children (Jer 7:31) to Moloch, god of the Ammonites and Phoenicians. To stop the abominable practices, King Josiah littered the site with human bones, dead criminals and animals, and other unclean things (2 Kings 23:10). It thereafter became a garbage dump where the city's waste and dead animals were burned continuously. Flies abounded, and their maggots covered the remains of carcasses. It "became the representative or image of the place of everlasting punishment, especially on account of its ever-burning fires."[27]

Next door to lake of fire. The rich man was sorely desperate from great thirst in the unbearable heat. *"And he cried and said, Father Abraham, have mercy on me, and send*

Lazarus, that he may dip the tip of his finger in water, and cool my tongue; for I am tormented in this flame" (Luke 16:24). The Greek word used for "flame" is *phlox*, which is the "gaseous part of fire," not the fire itself (*pyros*), showing that Gehenna is not the lake of fire, but is simply adjacent and so close to it that the heat and flames make it a place of torment.

The rich man's plea cannot be granted. *"But Abraham said, Son, remember that thou in thy lifetime receivedst thy good things, and likewise Lazarus evil things: but now he is comforted, and thou art tormented"* (Luke 16:25). Matthew Henry tells us: "This rich man had entirely devoted himself to the pleasures of the world of sense, was wholly taken up with them, and took up with them for his portion, and therefore was wholly unfit for the pleasures of the world of spirits; to such a carnal mind as his they would indeed be no pleasure, nor could he have any relish of them, and therefore he is of course excluded from them."[28]

Separated by a canyon. There is a second good reason, ostensibly physical. *"And beside all this, between us and you there is a great gulf fixed: so that they which would pass from hence to you cannot; neither can they pass to us, that would come from thence"* (Luke 16:26). A Jewish teaching Josephus quotes agrees with the Gospel account -- "...and not only so, but where they see the place of the fathers and of the just, even hereby are they punished; for a chaos deep and large is fixed between them; insomuch that a just man that hath compassion upon them cannot be admitted, nor can one that is unjust, if he were bold enough to attempt it, pass over it."[29]

A Jewish tradition has it that at the bottom of the impassable canyon separating *Gan Eden* and *Gehenna* is a river flowing with cool, refreshing waters. However, whenever anyone from *Gehenna* goes down and tries to scoop some water from the river, the water recedes! This is repeated endlessly at every attempt. That was why the rich man begged Abraham to send down Lazarus to dip his finger in the water for him. He was in front of the water, and yet was unable to refresh himself!

Luke gives us ample forewarning: *"There shall be weeping and gnashing of teeth, when ye shall see Abraham, and Isaac, and Jacob, and all the prophets, in the kingdom of God, and you yourselves thrust out"* (Luke 13:28).

Temporary holding places.

Both *Gan Eden* and *Gehenna*, the two regions of *Hades* (or *Sheol*), are only temporary dwelling places for the spirits of the dead. Josephus wrote that the saved will be in the Bosom of Abraham "while they wait for that rest and eternal new life in heaven, which is to succeed this region."[30]

The New Unger's Bible Dictionary wholly confirms this, calling Hades the "intermediate state." "The rich man, who is evidently still in Hades, is a representative case and describes the unjudged condition in the intermediate state of the wicked."[31]

The Jews believed they would be in *Hades* until they are raised from the dead. "This is the discourse concerning Hades, wherein the souls of all men are confined until a proper season, which God hath determined, when he will make a resurrection of all men from the dead, not procuring a transmigration of souls from one body to another, but raising again those very bodies."[32]

Restoration of all things. The dead will be in Hades until the restoration of all things. *"Repent, then, and turn to God, so that your sins may be wiped out, that times of refreshing may come from the Lord, and that he may send the Christ, who has been appointed for you -- even Jesus. He must remain in heaven until the time comes for God to restore everything, as he promised long ago through his holy prophets"* (Acts 3:19-22, NIV). Implicit in the verse is that the restoration will begin at the Second Coming of Christ.

The demons themselves know it. *"And, behold, they cried out, saying, What have we to do with thee, Jesus, thou Son of God? art thou come hither to torment us before the time?"* (Matt 8:29). Evidently, there is a timeframe, at the end of which – that is, after the second resurrection -- everyone, angels and men alike, will be judged.

From we read in the Scriptures, it appears that the elect saints, who will have become kings under Christ, the King of Kings during the Millennial Kingdom, will be members of the jury. *"Do ye not know that the saints shall judge the world? and if the world shall be judged by you, are ye unworthy to judge the smallest matters? Know ye not that we shall judge angels?"* (1 Cor 6:2-3a).

The second resurrection.

"But the rest of the dead lived not again until the thousand years were finished" (Rev 20:5). All remaining dead humans since the time of Adam will be resurrected after the Millennium. The oldest will have been dead for over 6,000 years!

The Jewish sages "believed that the body will be raised again; for although it be dissolved, it is not perished; for the earth receives its remains, and preserves them… but at the mighty sound of God the Creator, it will sprout up, and be raised in a clothed and glorious condition…for although it be dissolved for a time on account of the original transgression, it exists still, and is cast into the earth as into a potter's furnace, in order to be formed again…"[33] How? Most of those bodies have long, long ago disintegrated. How can they be reconstituted?

Cloned from DNA? The modern science of genetics seems to have the answer. An entire human being can be replicated or cloned from the DNA (deoxyribonucleic acid) in the nucleus of a single human cell smaller than a speck of dust! (The DNA carries the genes that give each organism its individual characteristics.)

From time to time, we see in the news stories of scientists finding tissues of extinct animals with the DNA intact, raising the prospect of restoring those species back to life. Similarly, long dead persons could be reconstructed from surviving DNA!

And "to everybody shall its own soul be restored"[34] It looks like the body, *neshamah,* soul, and spirit will all be reunited!

The Last Judgment.

"And I saw a great white throne, and him that sat on it, from whose face the earth and the heaven fled away; and there was found no place for them. And I saw the dead, small and great, stand before God; and the books were opened: and another book was opened, which is the book of life: and the dead were judged out of those things which were written in the books, according to their works. And the sea gave up the dead which were in it; and death and hell delivered up the dead which were in them: and they were judged every man according to their works. And death and hell were cast into the lake of fire. This is the second death. And whosoever was not found written in the book of life was cast into the lake of fire" (Rev 20:11-15).

8

The Light of Eternal Life

He will make your righteousness shine like the dawn, the justice of your cause like the noonday sun.

-- Psalm 37:6, NIV.

In their role as ministering spirits and guardians, how can the angels in the stars distinguish the heirs of salvation they are supposed to protect from among the billions of other people on earth? On the other side of the coin, how can Satan and his demons pinpoint the righteous individuals they must pay special attention to in leading astray from salvation?

We will do well to hark back to the very beginning of the universe. *"In the beginning God created the heaven and the earth. And the earth was without form, and void; and darkness was upon the face of the deep. And the Spirit of God moved upon the face of the waters. And God said, Let there be light: and there was light. And God saw the light, that it was good: and God divided the light from the darkness"* (Gen 1:1-4).

Throughout the Bible, light represents goodness and truth. The Scriptures speak of light as the symbol of God's presence and righteous activity. In addition, after the creation of man, light became a symbol of purity and holiness.

Literal and figurative

The word "light" in the Scriptures is used both literally and figuratively. In the literal sense, it means illumination, brightness or radiance, the opposite of darkness. As a figure of speech, light has to do with the spiritual, moral and mental aspects of life.

Light can signify spiritual enlightenment. *"In thy light .... we see light"* (Ps 36:9); *"The life was the light of men"* (John 1:4).

In a moral sense, light pertains to man's attitude to truth, as we see in Job 24:13,16 – *"They are of those that rebel against the light; they know not the ways thereof, nor abide in the paths thereof... In the dark they dig through houses, which they had marked for themselves in the daytime: they know not the light."* Isaiah 5:20 describes a moral confusion and blindness that cannot distinguish light from darkness. *"Woe unto them that call evil good, and good evil; that put darkness for light, and light for darkness; that put bitter for sweet, and sweet for bitter!"*

Applied to a man's mental condition, light is said to come to the intellect or mind through divine instruction. *"The entrance of thy words giveth light; it giveth understanding unto the simple"* (Ps 119:130).

God is light

The origin of light is found in the very nature of God, who, besides being the Creator of light, is also light, according to John. *"This then is the message which we have heard of him, and declare unto you, that God is light, and in him is no darkness at all"* (1 John 1:5).

For this reason, God's appearance is described as light. *"But ye are a chosen generation, a royal priesthood, an holy nation, a peculiar people; that ye should shew forth the praises of him who hath called you out of darkness into his marvellous light"* (1 Peter 2:9).

Clothed with light.

In terms men can understand, the psalmist says God is clad with light. *"Bless the LORD, O my soul. O LORD my God, thou art very great; thou art clothed with honour and majesty. Who coverest thyself with light as with a garment: who stretchest out the heavens like a curtain"* (Ps 104:1-2).

And, considering His holiness and perfection, God is the one *"Who only hath immortality, dwelling in the light which no man can approach unto; whom no man hath seen, nor can see: to whom be honour and power everlasting. Amen"* (1 Tim 6:16).

Angels are light

The angels, as we have already seen earlier, are also lights, being sons of the Father of lights (James 1:17). They are also the shining stars in heaven (Rev 1:20a, etc.).

Fiery figures.

Some angels are ablaze and radiant with light. *"And I saw another mighty angel come down from heaven, clothed with a cloud: and a rainbow was upon his head, and his face was as it were the sun, and his feet as pillars of fire"* (Rev 10:1).

"Then I lifted up mine eyes, and looked, and behold a certain man clothed in linen, whose loins were girded with fine gold of Uphaz: His body also was like the beryl, and his face as the appearance of lightning, and his eyes as lamps of fire, and his arms and his feet like in colour to polished brass, and the voice of his words like the voice of a multitude" (Dan 10:5-6).

For godly eyes only?

The vision of the angelic being Daniel saw was not visible to the men with him. They only felt its terrible presence. *"And I Daniel alone saw the vision: for the men that were with me saw not the vision; but a great quaking fell upon them, so that they fled to hide themselves"* (Dan 10:7).

Invisible to ordinary men.

The men with Saul (Paul), who were on their way to Damascus to arrest Christians, were similarly in the dark as to what was happening. *"And as he journeyed, he came near Damascus: and suddenly there shined round about him a light from heaven: And he fell to the earth, and heard a voice saying unto him, Saul, Saul, why persecutest thou me? ...And the men which journeyed with him stood speechless, hearing a voice, but seeing no man"* (Acts 9:3-4,7). It appears that ordinary men cannot see celestial beings or even their lights. It looks like only righteous men and those specially favored by God can see the light of their manifestations.

Seen only spiritually?

Abraham recognized angels on sight. It is a mystery how he instantly knew that the three men who came to visit him were angels of the LORD. What did he see in them? *"And the LORD appeared unto him in the plains of Mamre: and he sat in the tent door in the heat of the day; And he lift up his eyes and looked, and, lo, three men stood by him: and when he saw them, he ran to meet them from the tent door, and bowed himself toward the ground"* (Gen 18:1-2).

Abraham's nephew, Lot, whom the angels also saw to warn about the coming destruction of Sodom and Gomorrah, likewise recognized the angels immediately. *"And there came two angels to Sodom at even; and Lot sat in the gate of Sodom: and Lot seeing them rose up to meet them; and he bowed himself with his face toward the ground"* (Gen 19:1).

The Son of God.

It was probably Christ who appeared to Daniel -- some 600 years before His birth as the Messiah. The description is virtually identical to that in Revelation.

In a vision of the end-times, John partially echoes the description of the angel Daniel saw, specially the eyes and feet. *"And in the midst of the seven candlesticks one like unto the Son of man, clothed with a garment down to the foot, and girt about the paps with a golden girdle. His head and his hairs were white like wool, as white as snow; and his eyes were as a flame of fire; And his feet like unto fine brass, as if they burned in a furnace; and his voice as the sound of many waters"* (Rev 1:13-15).

The same portrayal is repeated in the succeeding chapter. *"And unto the angel of the church in Thyatira write; These things saith the Son of God, who hath his eyes like unto a flame of fire, and his feet are like fine brass"* (Rev 2:18).

The "light of the world"

Christ, as God's mediator in creation, generated all life in the universe and, with life, gave men the unique light of reason. *"In him was life; and the life was the light of men"* (John 1:4). What is more, He illuminates those who are dead in their sins, *"Wherefore he saith, Awake thou that sleepest, and arise from the dead, and Christ shall give thee light"* (Eph 5:14).

Christ thus rightfully referred to Himself as light. *"I am come a light into the world, that whosoever believeth on me should not abide in darkness"* (John 12:46). He lights up all mankind. *"Then spake Jesus again unto them, saying, I am the light of the world: he that followeth me shall not walk in darkness, but shall have the light of life"* (John 8:12).

His light that shone on the world, though, would be but for a brief period. *"As long as I am in the world, I am the light of the world"* (John 9:5). He told His disciples not to pass up the opportunity while He was with them. *"Then Jesus said unto them, Yet a little while is the light with you. Walk while ye have the light, lest darkness come upon you: for he that walketh in darkness knoweth not whither he goeth"* (John 12:35).

"Light of the Gentiles."

Some six hundred years earlier, Isaiah foreshadowed the Messiah as a "light" for the Gentiles. *"I the LORD have called thee in righteousness, and will hold thine hand, and will keep thee, and give thee for a covenant of the people, for a light of the Gentiles"* (Isa 42:6). Nonetheless, Israel would still be first and foremost in God's plan, Gentiles only second. *"And he said, It is a light thing that thou shouldest be my servant to raise up the tribes of Jacob, and to restore the preserved of Israel: I will also give thee for a light to the Gentiles, that thou mayest be my salvation unto the end of the earth"* (Isa 49:6).

The prophecy was confirmed when Christ was born. *"And, behold, there was a man in Jerusalem, whose name was Simeon; and the same man was just and devout, waiting for the consolation of Israel: and the Holy Ghost was upon him. And it was revealed unto him by the Holy Ghost, that he should not see death, before he had seen the Lord's Christ. And he came by the Spirit into the temple: and when the parents brought in the child Jesus, to do for him after the custom of the law, Then took he him up in his arms, and blessed God, and said, Lord, now lettest thou thy servant depart in peace, according to thy word:*

For mine eyes have seen thy salvation, Which thou hast prepared before the face of all people; A light to lighten the Gentiles, and the glory of thy people Israel" (Luke 2:25-32).

The "Transfiguration."

Christ was suffused with blinding light in a supernatural event called the "Transfiguration." *"And after six days Jesus taketh Peter, James, and John his brother, and bringeth them up into an high mountain apart, And was transfigured before them: and his face did shine as the sun, and his raiment was white as the light. And, behold, there appeared unto them Moses and Elias talking with him"* (Matt 17:1-3).

God glorified Him. *"For he received from God the Father honour and glory, when there came such a voice to him from the excellent glory, This is my beloved Son, in whom I am well pleased. And this voice which came from heaven we heard, when we were with him in the holy mount"* (2 Peter 1:17-18).

Light of the Church

The pure, spotless religion God gave Abraham is radiant with light. *"And there appeared a great wonder in heaven; a woman clothed with the sun, and the moon under her feet, and upon her head a crown of twelve stars"* (Rev 12:1). As we have discussed earlier, the "woman" represents the Abrahamic faith; the "sun," righteousness; "moon," idolatry; and the "twelve stars," the twelve tribes of Israel.

Light of Zion. Isaiah 60:1-3 prophesies: *"Arise, shine; for thy light is come, and the glory of the LORD is risen upon thee. For, behold, the darkness shall cover the earth, and gross darkness the people: but the LORD shall arise upon thee, and his glory shall be seen upon thee. And the Gentiles shall come to thy light, and kings to the brightness of thy rising."* Explains the *International Standard Bible Encyclopaedia*: "The church.-- Zion was to 'shine' because her `light had come' (Isa 60:1). The Gentiles were to come to her light (60:3). Her mission as the enlightener of the world was symbolized in the ornamentations of her priesthood. The Urim of the high priest's breastplate signified light, and the name itself is but the plural form of the Hebrew 'or. It stood for revelation, and thummim for truth."[1]

The prophecy has not taken place yet. It appears to presage a future convergence of Gentiles toward the light of the Abrahamic faith of Zion, the root and progenitor of the Judeo-Christian religion that we have today. Is it a prophecy of a global revival wherein Gentiles will flock to the church of Zion?

Light of the Gospel. The Gospel, or the good news of salvation in Christ, despite Satan's efforts to prevent men from understanding it, similarly spreads light. *"In whom the god of this world hath blinded the minds of them which believe not, lest the light of the glorious gospel of Christ, who is the image of God, should shine unto them"* (2 Cor 4:4).

Enlightened men

Like God, Christ, and the angels, godly men can shine with the divine light of holiness, too.

Moses. After communing with God on Mount Sinai, Moses came down from the mountain with his face shining. *"And it came to pass, when Moses came down from mount Sinai with the two tables of testimony in Moses' hand, when he came down from the mount, that Moses wist not that the skin of his face shone while he talked with him. And when Aaron and all the children of Israel saw Moses, behold, the skin of his face shone; and they were afraid to come nigh him"* (Ex 34:29-30).

John the Baptist. Christ said His cousin John, who prepared the way for Him, was one bright light. *"Ye sent unto John, and he bare witness unto the truth. But I receive not testimony from man: but these things I say, that ye might be saved. He was a burning and a shining light: and ye were willing for a season to rejoice in his light"* (John 5:33-35).

Garments of light

As God clothes Himself with light, so too can men wear light – in more ways than one. Let us see how we can do it.

Righteousness is light.

The light from the sun is used as a simile for righteousness. *"Commit thy way unto the LORD; trust also in him; and he shall bring it to pass. And he shall bring forth thy righteousness as the light, and thy judgment as the noonday"* (Ps 37:5-6).

The light of righteousness can be worn like a garment, Job says. *"I put on righteousness, and it clothed me: my judgment was as a robe and a diadem"* (Job 29:14). The psalmist also sings, *"Let thy priests be clothed with righteousness; and let thy saints shout for joy"* (Ps 132:9). Isaiah, for his part, sagely says, *"And righteousness shall be the girdle of his loins, and faithfulness the girdle of his reins"* (Isa 11:5).

Salvation is light.

Light can also mean "salvation." *"The LORD is my light and my salvation; whom shall I fear? the LORD is the strength of my life; of whom shall I be afraid?"* (Ps 27:1).

Like righteousness, salvation can be worn as clothing. *"Now therefore arise, O LORD God, into thy resting place, thou, and the ark of thy strength: let thy priests, O LORD God, be clothed with salvation, and let thy saints rejoice in goodness"* (2 Chron 6:41). Furthermore, *"I will also clothe her priests with salvation: and her saints shall shout aloud for joy"* (Ps 132:16).

Righteousness and salvation.

Righteousness and salvation can be worn together. *"I will greatly rejoice in the LORD, my soul shall be joyful in my God; for he hath clothed me with the garments of salvation, he hath covered me with the robe of righteousness, as a bridegroom decketh himself with ornaments, and as a bride adorneth herself with her jewels"* (Isa 61:10).

It becomes evident that "light," "sun," "righteousness," and "salvation" are at times used synonymously in the Bible, specially when being worn like garments.

Wearing Christ.

And, surprise!, we can also wear Christ. *"For as many of you as have been baptized into Christ have put on Christ"* (Gal 3:27). We *"have put on the new self, which is being renewed in knowledge in the image of its Creator"* (Col 3:10, NIV).

From being sinners we must wear the righteousness and holiness of a new person in Christ after we are cleansed. *"And that ye put on the new man, which after God is created in righteousness and true holiness"* (Eph 4:24).

Saints shine bright

The light of eternal life is planted to grow in all those who will be heirs of salvation. *"Light is sown like seed for the righteous"* (Ps 97:11a, NASU).

"Children of light." Biblical writers call the saints the "children of light." In John 12:36a -- *"While ye have light, believe in the light, that ye may be the children of light."* In Luke 16:8 -- *"And the lord commended the unjust steward, because he had done wisely: for the children of this world are in their generation wiser than the children of light."* In Ephesians 5:8 -- *"For ye were sometimes darkness, but now are ye light in the Lord: walk as children of light."*

"Lights in the world." Christ, "the light of the world," said the saints are just like Him. *"Ye are the light of the world"* (Matt 5:14a). As such, we are expected to be seen by the rest of the world as shining exemplars and role models in the faith. *"That ye may be blameless and harmless, the sons of God, without rebuke, in the midst of a crooked and perverse nation, among whom ye shine as lights in the world"* (Phil 2:15).

How saints shine.

The Savior taught the disciples how to be filled with light. *"The light of the body is the eye: if therefore thine eye be single, thy whole body shall be full of light"* (Matt 6:22). Accordingly, if we single-mindedly focus our eyes on obeying the will of God and thereby walk righteously, we will be covered with light.

How does this happen? We have the insight of the Hebrew sages to enlighten us. Let us refresh our memories with something we have read in the previous chapter.

Supernal light. According to ancient Jewish wisdom, "The *nephesh* possesses in itself no light and cannot out of its own being engender it, and for this reason it is in close connection and deeply enmeshed with its body. The *ruah* rides upon the *nephesh*, dominates it, and enlightens it with supernal glory, as much as it can bear; this *nephesh* is the throne of the *ruah*. The *neshamah* produces the *ruah*, rules over it, and sheds upon it the light of life. The *ruah* depends entirely upon the *neshamah* and it is lit up by its light and nourished by its celestial food, while the *nephesh* is similarly dependent on the *ruah*."[2]

Let us rephrase that more concisely. Only the *neshamah* inherently possesses heavenly light, with which it lights up the *ruach*, which in turn enlightens the *nephesh*.

Identifying light. That being the case, all saints therefore shine with the divine light of eternal life! Is this how the angels recognize the heirs of salvation they zealously guard and protect? And, in the same way, is this how the demons pinpoint the righteous people they want to tempt and lead astray?

Darkness: the other side

Whereas light is the symbol and expression of holiness and eternal life, darkness is the universal symbol and condition of sin and death. Darkness represents error, evil, and the works of the devil. This must be why God separated light and darkness from the very beginning. *"And God saw the light, that it was good: and God divided the light from the darkness"* (Gen 1:4).

Look at what happens when people eschew righteousness. *"But if thine eye be evil, thy whole body shall be full of darkness. If therefore the light that is in thee be darkness, how great is that darkness!"* (Matt 6:23).

No light in wicked men.

The light in evil men, if ever they had any to begin with, becomes extinguished. *"Yea, the light of the wicked shall be put out, and the spark of his fire shall not shine. The light shall be dark in his tabernacle, and his candle shall be put out with him"* (Job 18:5-6).

Regrettably, evildoers much prefer darkness to light. *"And this is the condemnation, that light is come into the world, and men loved darkness rather than light, because their deeds were evil. For every one that doeth evil hateth the light, neither cometh to the light, lest his deeds should be reproved. But he that doeth truth cometh to the light, that his deeds may be made manifest, that they are wrought in God"* (John 3:19-21).

Paul cautioned Christians not to associate with pagans and idolaters, whom he likened to darkness. *"Be ye not unequally yoked together with unbelievers: for what fellowship hath righteousness with unrighteousness? and what communion hath light with darkness?"* (2 Cor 6:14).

Sin is nakedness

Those who have little or no faith at all in God and His Son will eventually find themselves spiritually naked. *"Behold, I come as a thief. Blessed is he that watcheth, and keepeth his garments, lest he walk naked, and they see his shame"* (Rev 16:15).

It looks like the lake of fire will be filled with spiritually naked people. *"Hell is naked before him, and destruction hath no covering"* (Job 26:6).

Adam and Eve.

Were Adam and Eve, who had been created sinless and intended to live forever, not ashamed of their nakedness because they were clothed with the light of eternal life? *"And they were both naked, the man and his wife, and were not ashamed"* (Gen 2:25).

After they sinned by disobeying God, did the light of eternal life covering them suddenly go out, exposing their nakedness? *"And the eyes of them both were opened, and they knew that they were naked..."* (Gen 3:7a).

The Garden paradigm.

If that was the untold side-story in the Garden of Eden, then it was the primordial model -- the paradigm -- for all mankind: Obey God and be clothed with the light of eternal life, and live forever in Paradise. The alternative: disobey and be stripped naked, and be cast out from the presence of God into a terrible place of never-ending destruction. *"And they shall go forth, and look upon the carcases of the men that have transgressed against me: for their worm shall not die, neither shall their fire be quenched; and they shall be an abhorring unto all flesh"* (Isa 66:24; cf. Mark 9:43-48).

Star lights extinguished

Ironically, Lucifer, whose name means "light-bearer," has become the "prince of darkness." Now also known as Satan, he aspired to be above all other angels, the "stars" in heaven. *"For thou hast said in thine heart, I will ascend into heaven, I will exalt my throne above the stars of God: I will sit also upon the mount of the congregation, in the sides of the north"* (Isa 14:13).

Empty north. Satan apparently succeeded in seducing most of the angels (stars) in the northern region of heaven. That quadrant of the sky is practically empty, devoid of stars, says Job in 26:7a: *"He stretcheth out the north over the empty place..."*

Incredibly, astronomers have discovered that the area north of the axis of the Earth is indeed nearly empty! An article in the November 27, 1981, issue of *Science* magazine reported: "The recently announced 'hole in space,' a 300 million-light-year-gap in the distribution of galaxies, has taken cosmologists by surprise. But three very deep core samples in the Northern Hemisphere, lying in the general direction of the constellation Bootes, showed striking gaps in the red shift distribution."[3]

Did the lights of the stars in the northern quarter of heaven go out when most of the angels there sinned by joining Satan? *"And his tail drew the third part of the stars of heaven, and did cast them to the earth"* (Rev 12:4a).

Cosmic harmony

After the sixth day of creation, *"God saw every thing that he had made, and, behold, it was very good"* (Gen 1:31a). All things in the universe were according to His will and satisfaction. There was perfect harmony in heaven and earth.

The immortal angels in the stars shone with the light of eternal life. But the lights of a third of them flickered and went out when they went against the will of God. Large parts of the firmament were darkened. Suddenly, there was disharmony in heaven and, through the mischief of Satan, on earth.

"Northern lights."

Cosmic harmony has to be restored. The angel Gabriel told Daniel: *"And they that be wise shall shine as the brightness of the firmament; and they that turn many to righteousness as the stars for ever and ever"* (Dan 12:3). The saints will shine like the stars! Will some 100 million brilliant stars soon radiantly shine with the light of eternal life in the northern sides, as well as in the other parts, of heaven?

"Thy will be done in earth, as it is in heaven" (Matt 6:10).

Appendix

One-third of one percent?

Cryptically, a distinct percentage that seemingly numbers the few chosen remnants vis-à-vis the rest of all the people has been uncovered in two veiled prophecies.

Joshua and Caleb.

Six hundred thousand Israelite men left Egypt in the Exodus. *"And the children of Israel journeyed from Rameses to Succoth, about six hundred thousand on foot that were men, beside children"* (Ex 12:37). The Hebrew word used for "thousand" is *eleph*, which can also mean "family." Hence, "600 thousand" can also be read as "600 families."

After forty years in the wilderness, of all the men aged 20 years and older who left Egypt, only two, Joshua and Caleb, representing two families, lived long enough to enter the Promised Land. Two families out of a total of 600 families is one-third of one percent. Does it prophetically point to the percentage of those who will be saved?

Gideon's 300.

Of the 32,000 Israelite volunteers, God picked just 300 men to secure victory with Gideon against the 135,000 Midianites and their allies. *"The LORD said to Gideon, 'With the three hundred men that lapped I will save you and give the Midianites into your hands....'"* (Judg 7:7a, NIV)

Assuming that, prophetically, the 32,000 are 32 billion men who will have lived from creation to the Last Judgment; the 22,000 who would not fight are 22 billion who will never have engaged in wars; the 10,000 who stayed to fight are 10 billion who will have fought in wars from creation to Armageddon; and the 300 are God's 300 million angels; then Gideon's 300 stand for approximately 1% of the 32,000 total.

If 100 of the 300 represent the saints who will replace the fallen angels, their number is thus one-third of 1% of all the people. Will this prove to be true? Time will tell.

Endnotes

1. Angels Up Close and Personal
1. Book of Enoch 43:1-2
2. Female, *New Exhaustive Strong's Numbers and Concordance*, 1994
3. Seraphim, *The New Unger's Bible Dictionary,*1988
4. Elder, *Fausset's Bible Dictionary,* 1998
5. Dan 4:13, *Barnes' Notes*, 1997
6. *Ibid.*
7. Angel, *International Standard Bible Encyclopaedia*, 1996
8. Angel, *Nelson's Illustrated Bible Dictionary*, 1986)
9. Angel, *International Standard Bible Encyclopaedia*, 1996
10. Archangel, Encarta Encyclopedia, 1993-2003
11. Louis Sperry Chafer, quoted by N.W. Hutchings and Bob Glaze, *Angels: From Genesis to Revelation,*1997, pp. 30-31

2. The Roles Angels Play
1. Angel, *International Standard Bible Encyclopaedia*, 1996
2. 1 Cor 7:14, *The Wycliffe Bible Commentary*, 1962
3. Angel, *Nelson's Illustrated Bible Dictionary*, 1986

3. Rebels and Renegades
1. 2 Peter 1:19-21, *Matthew Henry's Commentary on the Whole Bible: New Modern Edition*, 1991
2. Mercy Seat, *Fausset's Bible Dictionary*, 1998
3. Mercy Seat, *Nelson's Illustrated Bible Dictionary*, 1986
4. Dennis Petersen, *Unlocking the Mysteries of Creation*, 2002, p. 71
5. Satan, *Fausset's Bible Dictionary*, 1998
6. Adversary, *Nelson's Illustrated Bible Dictionary,*1986
7. Dragon, *Fausset's Bible Dictionary,*1998
8. Serpent, *International Standard Bible Encyclopaedia,*1996
9. Beelzebub; Gods, Pagan; *Nelson's Illustrated Bible Dictionary*, 1986
10. Beelzebul, *Fausset's Bible Dictionary,*1998
11. Belial, *International Standard Bible Encyclopaedia,*1996
12. Belial, *Fausset's Bible Dictionary,*1998
13. Azazel, *Biblesoft's New Exhaustive Strong's Numbers and Concordance with Expanded Greek-Hebrew Dictionary.* 1994
14. Azazel, *The New Unger's Bible Dictionary.* 1988
15. Devil, *Nelson's Illustrated Bible Dictionary,*1986

16. Prince, *op. cit.*
17. John 12:27-36. *Matthew Henry's Commentary on the Whole Bible: New Modern Edition*, 1991
18. John 12:31. *Barnes' Notes*, 1997
19. 2 Cor 4:1-7. *Matthew Henry's Commentary on the Whole Bible: New Modern Edition*, 1991
20. 2 Cor 4:4. *Barnes' Notes*, 1997
21. Eph 2:2, *op. cit.*
22. Devil, *Fausset's Bible Dictionary*, 1998
23. Satyr, *International Standard Bible Encyclopaedia*, 1996
24. Ashtoreth, *International Standard Bible Encyclopaedia*, 1996
25. Queen of Heaven, *Fausset's Bible Dictionary*, 1998
26. Ashtaroth, *Nelson's Illustrated Bible Dictionary*, 1986
27. Jude 7. *Barnes' Notes*, 1997
28. Psalm 68:18, *op. cit.*

4. Battleground Earth!
1. Fred Alan Wolf, *Space-Time and Beyond*, 1987, p. 145
2. Phil 2:10, *Barnes' Notes*, 1997

5. The Heirs of Heaven
1. Gehenna; Lake of Fire, *The New Unger's Bible Dictionary*, 1988
2. Resurrection, *op. cit.*
3. Flavius Josephus, quoted by J.R. Church, "Home of the Soul [The Human Brain, Part Two]," *Prophecy in the News*, March 1999, p. 11
4. *Ibid.*
5. *Ibid.*
6. Bob Ulrich, review of Bill Salus's book, *Isralestine, Prophecy in the News*, September 2008, p. 17
7. Rev 7:1-12, *Matthew Henry's Commentary on the Whole Bible: New Modern Edition*, 1991
8. Rick 'Aharon' Chaimberlin, "The Four Horsemen of the Apoclypse," *A Messianic Jewish Commentary on the Book of Revelation* (2002-2007), p. 30
9. Emil Gaverluk, quoted by Noah Hutchings and Bob Glaze, *Angels from Genesis to Revelation*, 1997, p. 13
10. Satan, *Fausset's Bible Dictionary, 1998*
11. Saint Augustine, "1. Of the creation of angels and men," *The City of God*, 5th century
12. Jan Marcussen. quoting Ellen G. White, 509th newsletter, Mid-July Y2K +10, p. 5

13. Cindy Jacobs, "Prophecy for the Philippines," quoted by mystiqueowl, March 16, 2011, Internet
14. Azazel, *The New Unger's Bible Dictionary*, 1988

6. Man's Manual for Survival
1. Law, *Fausset's Bible Dictionary*, 1998
2. *Ibid.*
3. Ten Commandments, *International Standard Bible Encyclopaedia*, 1996
4. *Ibid.*
5. Ten Commandments, *The New Unger's Bible Dictionary*.1988
6. Ten Commandments, *International Standard Bible Encyclopaedia*, 1996
7. *Ibid.*
8. *Ibid.*
9. Acts 15:20, *Barnes' Notes*, 1997
10. Acts 15:20, *The Wycliffe Bible Commentary*, 1962
11. *Ibid.*
12. *Ibid.*
13. Acts 15:20, *Barnes' Notes*, 1997
14. Chuck Missler, *Cosmic Codes*, 1999, revised 2004, p. 126
15. Grant Jeffrey, *The Signature of God*, 1996, p.205
16. Law, *Fausset's Bible Dictionary*,1998
17. Law, *Nelson's Illustrated Bible Dictionary*,1986
18. Images and Idols, *Hastings Encyclopedia of Religion and Ethics*, cited by Ralph Woodrow, *Babylon Mystery Religion*, 1981, p. 36
19. Icon, *Ecncylopaedia Britannica*
20. Iconoclastic Controversy, *op. cit.*
21. Iconoclasm, *Encarta Encylopedia*
22. Councils of Nicaea, *op. cit.*
23. Iconoclastic Controversy, *loc. cit.*
24. Iconoclasm, *op. cit.*
25. Fringes, *International Standard Bible Encyclopaedia*, 1996
26. Fringes, *Fausset's Bible Dictionary*,1998
27. Tallith, *Encyclopaedia Britannica*
28. Hair, *International Standard Bible Encyclopaedia*, 1996
29. Hair, *Fausset's Bible Dictionary*, 1998
30. Hair, *Nelson's Illustrated Bible Dictionary*,1986
31. Hair, *International Standard Bible Encyclopaedia*,1996
32. Lev 19:19-29, *Matthew Henry's Commentary on the Whole Bible: New Modern Edition*, 1991
33. Lev 19:26-28, *Barnes' Notes*, Electronic Database. 1997
34. Pentecost, *Fausset's Bible Dictionary*,1998

35. Feasts, *op. cit.*
36. Law, *Nelson's Illustrated Bible Dictionary*, 1986
37. *Ibid.*
38. Law, *Fausset's Bible Dictionary*, 1998
39. *Ibid.*
40. *Ibid.*
41. Priests, *Nelson's Illustrated Bible Dictionary*, 1986
42. Sacrificial Offerings, *The New Unger's Bible Dictionary*, 1988
43. Law, *International Standard Bible Encyclopaedia*, 1996

7. Secrets of the Soul and Spirit
1. Spirit, *The New Unger's Bible Dictionary*. 1988
2. Body, *International Standard Bible Encyclopaedia*, 1996
3. Spirit, *Fausset's Bible Dictionary*, 1998
4. Migene Gonzalez-Wippler, *A Kabbalah for the Modern World*, 1974, p. 149
5. Spirit, *Fausset's Bible Dictionary*, 1998
6. Spirit, *International Standard Bible Encyclopaedia*, 1996
7. Sheldon Z. Kramer, "Jewish Meditation," pp. 226-228
8. Migene Gonzalez-Wippler, *op. cit.*, p. 148
9. Jewish commentary on the Torah, quoted by J.R. Church, "Home of the Soul [The Human Brain, Part Three]," *Prophecy* in the News, April 1999, p. 16
10. Spirit, *The New Unger's Bible Dictionary*. 1988
11. Traducianism, *Wikipedia*, Internet
12. *Ibid.*
13. Eccl 12:1-7, *Matthew Henry's Commentary on the Whole Bible: New Modern Edition*, 1991
14. Jewish commentary on the Torah, *loc. cit.*
15. *Ibid.*
16. *Ibid.*
17. *Ibid.*
18. Hades, *International Standard Bible Encyclopaedia*, 1996
19. Josephus, quoted by J.R. Church, "Home of the Soul [The Human Brain, Part Two]," *Prophecy in the News*, March 1999, p. 10
20. Hades, *The New Unger's Bible Dictionary*. 1988
21. Luke 16:19-31, *Matthew Henry's Commentary on the Whole Bible: New Modern Edition*, 1991
22. Hades, *loc. cit.*
23. Luke 16:19-31, *loc. cit.*
24. Heavens, *International Standard Bible Encyclopaedia*, 1996

25. William J. Morford, "Seven Heavens," Power New Testament revealing Jewish Roots, Internet
26. Josephus, *op. cit.,* pp. 10-11
27. Gehenna, *The New Unger's Bible Dictionary,* 1988
28. Luke 16:19-31, *loc. cit.*
29. Josephus, *op. cit.,* p. 11
30. *Op. cit.,* p. 10
31. Hades, *loc. cit.*
32. Josephus, *op. cit.,* p. 11
33. *Ibid.*
34. *Ibid.*

8. The Light of Eternal Life
1. Light, *International Standard Bible Encyclopaedia,* 1996
2. Jewish commentary on the Torah, quoted by J.R. Church, "Home of the Soul [The Human Brain, Part Three," *Prophecy* in the News, April 1999, p. 16
3. Mitchell Waldrop, "Delving the Hole in Space," *Science,* 27 Nov. 1981

www.ingramcontent.com/pod-product-compliance
Lightning Source LLC
Chambersburg PA
CBHW071503040426
42444CB00008B/1476